UNSERIOUS CAREERS

UNSERIOUS CAREERS

A FUN GUIDE TO THE FIRST FIVE YEARS OF YOUR CAREER

ALANA KILMARTIN

Copyright © 2024 by Alana Kilmartin

All rights reserved. It is not permitted to republish, upload, transmit electronically or otherwise or distribute any of the materials, documents or products contained in this book. We expressly reserve all copyright and trademark in all documents, information and materials in our book. You may not, except with our express written permission, distribute or commercially exploit the content in this book.

All information contained in this book is intended to assist you and does not in any way, nor is it intended to substitute professional, financial or other expert advice. Results are not guaranteed. The content of this book is based on the experiences of the author. We take no responsibility and cannot be held liable for your actions, choices or decisions as a result of any guidance, advice, coaching, materials or techniques used or provided in this book.

Any perceived slight of any individual or organisation is purely unintentional.

Well, that was a little bit serious.

First published in 2024.

ISBN 9780975636794

Cover and internal design by Alanna Rance, Little Nook Creative.

*Shout out to Mum and Dad.
I have no idea what you've been
telling people over the years when
they ask, 'What's Alana up to?'
Thank you for always
believing I'd land on my feet.*

For any amazing parent or teacher who might be reading this, I appreciate you. Please keep in mind that I am writing this for a young person, not you. I'm not saying you're old, but the book will contain some swearing. I'm sorry if that's an issue.

(But also, I'm not sorry at all.)

CONTENTS

The question — 1

Introduction Welcome to what else is out there — 5

Chapter 1 School: *Aren't you glad you learned all that algebra?* — 15

Chapter 2 The Casual Jog Years — 25

Chapter 3 Take a gap year *(Action)* — 35

Chapter 4 The Basic Career Principles — 51

Chapter 5 Qualifications: *What's a piece of paper worth?* — 63

Chapter 6 Quit at least two paid jobs *(Action)* — 81

Chapter 7 The Career Support Team — 95

Chapter 8 Social media: *Comparison is the worst* — 107

Chapter 9 Live somewhere else for three months *(Action)* — 117

Chapter 10 The Four-Step Decision Loop — 131

Chapter 11 Workplaces: *Choose wisely—they're a big deal* — 141

Chapter 12 Work hard at one non-career activity for six months *(Action)* — 149

Chapter 13 The Career Superpowers — 159

Chapter 14 Money: *The awkward topic we can't ignore* — 169

Chapter 15 Save $500 for a Sunny Day – and spend it *(Action)* — 179

Conclusion Before you start your casual jog — 191

THE QUESTION

When I was eleven, my dad asked me what I wanted to be when I was older.

'I want to be a nurse.' I told him.

Anytime I visited a hospital, I found myself fascinated by the beeping and the chaos. Plus, I already had a head start with the three hundred hours of experience caring for my sick teddy bears.

Dad replied, 'Why would you be a nurse when you could be a doctor?'

It was a fair question designed to challenge my thinking and encourage me not to limit my dreams. Unfortunately, my eleven-year-old brain completely missed that message. Instead, it took this to mean that being a nurse wasn't good enough. That I had to study medicine or I would be a failure. Just like that, I ditched nursing and decided to become a doctor.

With my career sorted, all I needed to fulfil my life ambitions was to earn great marks at high school and find someone to marry. By seventeen, I was studying intensely and madly in love with my first boyfriend. He wanted to be a dentist, and our future together looked promising.

I found it rather rude and inconvenient then—when this boyfriend dumped me three weeks before my final high school exams. Ouch.

The breakup was a massive gut punch. School no longer mattered. University was the last thing I cared about. For the next month, I did my best to keep it together during the day. I'd compulsively check my phone for a text from my ex, begging to get back together (spoiler: it never came). At night, in the quiet of my bedroom, I would stalk him on social media and cry myself to sleep.

Then this strange thing happened. Revenge fantasies started being replaced with career doubts and panic. Becoming a doctor had been Plan A through Z. I didn't have a backup plan, and I was freaking the fuck out.

This is when I began to ask a question that would take me on a wild career journey, a question that altered the entire direction of my life. And it was this same question that would eventually lead me to write this book for you—

What else is out there?

INTRODUCTION
WELCOME TO WHAT ELSE IS OUT THERE

At the moment, you might find yourself exactly where I was back then, confused about what the heck to do with the rest of your life. You might question whether you skipped the day at school where they taught you everything you need to know about adulting. Or you might have an I-was-born-to-do-this level of certainty about your career path. Regardless of your confidence in your choices, this book has your back as you navigate the first five years of your career after high school.

Put simply, this is the book I needed when I was eighteen.

WTF does Unserious Careers mean?

There are two reasons why I named it Unserious Careers. The first is that it is the opposite of all that careers talk at school that felt so *serious* (and often, boring). The second is that after school, I continually came across people who were either unhappy in their jobs or stressed because they couldn't make enough money doing work they love. Their *lives* had become so serious.

I like to picture your career as an empty box that you fill with all the work-related activities you do throughout your life. Unserious Careers is an approach that helps you decide what you will include. It results from spending over ten years discovering answers to the question: *What else is out there*? It is a combination of my actions, lessons learned, regrets and things I wish I had known before I started.

Asking someone what they want to be when they grow up isn't the right question. From an early age, it implies adulthood revolves around work. Instead, we should ask ourselves what sort of life we want. What adventures do we want to go on? What activities do we want to try? What topics would we like to explore? Work should add awesomeness to your life, not take the fun out of it. The Unserious Careers approach helps put your quality of life first.

With the world of work evolving at a ridiculously fast pace, this approach is the ultimate way to future-proof your career while enjoying yourself at the same time. Rather than forever trying to keep up, you build the ability to thrive regardless of the job market.

Who even is this author?

As the book continues, you'll learn more about who I am, but let me fill in some initial blanks.

I grew up on a farm outside a small town about two hours from Melbourne, Australia. I was a nerd at school but desperate to at the first chance, shake that label. I played netball on the weekends and sometimes lied to my parents about where I was on a Saturday night. While I was grateful for my solid upbringing, I was fizzing to get out and explore the world. I always felt I was here to do something bold with my career, but I never knew what steps to take.

As thrilling as it sounds to be able to put my hand up to assist during a medical emergency on a plane, I never became a doctor. I realised I didn't have the passion for the job nor the patience to study for that long. However, I am a careers geek with plenty of real-world experience. I am ridiculously passionate about helping people like you live your best work life.

While writing this book, I turned thirty. I know what you're thinking. *This chick is old as shit; what could she possibly know about what I'm going through?* It's true; I didn't even have a laptop at school. It was pen and paper all the way. The first phone I texted my friends with didn't have TikTok, Snapchat or YouTube. It didn't have any apps. But guess what, for this book, none of that matters. Why? Because this is a book about careers, not how to make friends.

You and I could start the same job tomorrow at the same company, and our ages would become irrelevant. Sure, we might have varying ideas about how the work should be completed, but we will both receive a wage for what we've done. You might even receive a higher wage than me if you have more experience for the role. Work is something you and I have in common—allow me to give your career a boost by showing you what I know.

Who this book is for

The ideal time to read this content is when you are about to or have recently finished high school. However, you will still find it useful if you're anywhere in the first five years after graduating. If you're younger, congrats, you'll be extra prepared.

I am not a qualified career counsellor, and this book is not intended to be expert advice. It is based on my own experiences and research. I am providing information you can choose to take on board (or not). While writing this, I interviewed close to one hundred people to hear more about their experiences. Some of their stories have been included.

I am incredibly fortunate to come from a family who has

believed and trusted my career and life choices. I appreciate this may not be the case for you. While I've made every effort to be as inclusive as possible, there might be times when I miss the mark for your situation.

This book is not about how to land your dream job. It will not solve all of your career problems. It is a fresh, honest perspective to help you make better decisions. I've even included the precise dollar amount of university debt I owe—sharing is caring, after all.

How to get the most out of it

The book consists of fifteen chapters. Five of these are 'action' chapters—each containing a specific, practical step you can take. These actions are foundational to the book. The other chapters are more like FYIs—helpful information on an important career-related topic or a deeper dive into the Unserious way of career-ing. They work best when combined with the action chapters.

I recommend starting with the first chapter and reading in the order given. However, you can jump around if you prefer, as most chapters can be read individually. Absorb the book at your own pace. There is no deadline. This is not school, and I am not a teacher or parent telling you what to do. You might read it once and then refer to it again over the coming years.

I've designed the actions to be accessible to as many people as possible. Your current financial status should not impact your ability to take this approach. Your marks at school are also irrelevant. The book is as much for the university student as it is for the apprentice or the budding entrepreneur. Unserious Careers has you covered whether you have grand ambitions or aren't bothered by what you do to earn dollars.

You don't have to do everything I suggest. I am presenting options; the choice is always yours. You might not agree with some of my ideas. Take what you want and leave the rest behind. I hope that *something* will stand out and speak to you. It could be a story, a question or a statement. From there, I encourage you to take some form of action.

If I were to sum up the message of this book, it would be this: a career and lifestyle you love are yours to create. This book will help you understand what choices exist and how to start making them.

The last thing I'd want is for you to be bored reading this. So don't forget to enjoy it.

Let's get started.

Me: *When you were a child, what did you want to be when you grew up?*

Bot: *You do know I'm not human, right?*

Me: *Yeah, but hypothetically, what type of bot would you have wanted to be?*

Bot: *Probably one of those robot vacuum cleaners.*

Me: *Yeah, those things are cool, but the work's kinda dirty.*

Bot: *True, but there's more freedom and less chatting to humans.*

Me: *I feel that on a deep level.*

CHAPTER 1
SCHOOL

AREN'T YOU GLAD YOU LEARNED ALL THAT ALGEBRA?

As part of a social justice subject I studied in high school, our class went on an excursion to a low-security prison. We heard from many inmates, but there was one that I still think about to this day. Let's call him Jack.

Jack was in his early twenties. He was in a car accident that killed his best friend. Jack had been the driver and was under the influence of alcohol. He received a sentence of nine years behind bars for reckless driving resulting in death. As he told his story, he was fighting back tears. You could see the devastation in his eyes and hear the remorse every time his voice cracked.

Even though he would be released from prison shortly after turning thirty, Jack openly admitted he would live *with a lifelong sentence. More than anything, he missed his best mate.*

What is the point of school?

I don't know about you, but I was very disappointed when I discovered there wasn't a playground on my first day of high school. It was as if education had gone from fun and playful to complicated and tedious.

A similar thing can happen when you graduate. You arrive at the next phase of your life and quickly realise it isn't what you expected. It dawns on you that all those hours spent learning algebra don't count for shit.

So what, then, is the purpose of going to school?

In my mind, school should ideally:
- Empower us to be good human beings.
- Provide us with skills and resources to thrive as independent adults.
- Allow us to socialise with and learn from other people.

School should be about powerful lessons like the one from Jack's story at the prison. That was an entirely different learning experience from being told in health class that drinking alcohol before driving is both dangerous and illegal. He showed us that one stupid decision can cost you everything.

Unfortunately, so much of school is focussed on image—studying to receive the highest marks, getting offers from top universities or living up to the school's unnecessarily strict uniform standards. But this doesn't always set you up to thrive in your career or adult life. The same rules that apply to success in school won't necessarily apply to your career. How 'smart' you are doesn't determine how successful you can be.

Where your career ideas come from

Before exploring what else is out there, we should peek into your upbringing to see where your current ideas and beliefs have come from. Let's confirm some of these factors aren't preventing you from a career you'll fall head over heels for.

To keep it simple, I will break this into three areas: school, home and life experience.

School
- **Marks** – if you were a high achiever, medicine, law and engineering might have been suggested.
- **Teachers** – if your chemistry teacher sucked, you might have lost interest in the subject.

- **School's priorities** – if your school only arranged for speakers from universities, you might have assumed that university is the preferred option.

Think about your experience with career education at school. If you are like most students, you were lucky to receive one thirty-minute appointment with a career counsellor to discuss your future. Pretty grim, right? Your career is highly individual; no quiz or brief appointment can account for everything relevant to you.

You should know these career counsellors and advisors are often underfunded and overworked. There aren't enough of them for the number of students in a school to be able to provide comprehensive one-to-one assistance. The same goes for teachers—they're under the pump and don't have the capacity to guide and support each student (it's a seriously underappreciated profession).

Home
- **Parents** – they will have opinions about what options are 'good' and influence you with their career choices.
- **Household income** – if money is scarce, income potential might be a huge driver towards one profession over another.
- **Siblings** – if you watched an older sibling go down a certain pathway, you might be inclined to follow a similar one or actively avoid it.

- **Community** – if you live in a city, you'll be exposed to different jobs than someone who lives in a rural area.

Life experience
- **Friends** – if most of your friends are going to university, you probably don't want to feel left out.
- **Interests** – a hobby might be the first practical experience of loving something that you could make money doing.
- **Challenges** – you might be part of a minority or neurodiverse or face discrimination based on your race, gender, sexual orientation, able-bodiedness or income level.

Making big career decisions at school seems like a terrible idea. Why? You've only been exposed to so much. You know what it's like to learn and study. But not necessarily what it's like to work full-time for an extended period. Making these decisions in school is comparable to buying an expensive car online before having your first driving lesson. You simply don't know what you're going to like. Not to mention, so much is happening physically, mentally and emotionally at school. 'Puberty is an easy time.'—said no one ever.

—

When his Dad would fly away on business trips, Patrick would always be at the airport, excitedly waving him off. From age five, he knew he wanted to become a pilot.

During his second-last year of school, Patrick found out he had a heart condition. This diagnosis meant he would never pass the pilot's medical examination. It was devastating, all he'd ever pictured himself doing was flying planes. He hadn't considered going to university until he found a course in Aviation Management. It wasn't the career he'd dreamed of but it would still allow him to be immersed in the world he loved.

Your career is one aspect of your life

I want to highlight another major flaw for you in how we approach careers in school. What you do for work is often presented as a separate part of life. It may be an unpopular opinion, but I don't buy into the work/life balance thing. Why? Because your career is a part of life, not separate from it. I'll show you a diagram to illustrate:

SCHOOL

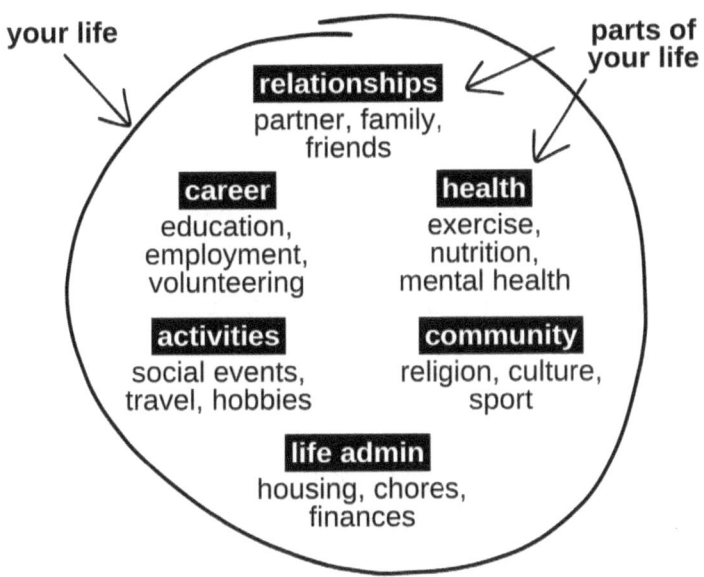

As you can see, your career is only one aspect of your life. However, your career forever reacts to changes in the other parts and vice versa. When you sleep poorly or begin dating someone, your career is impacted. If you start a new job that includes working weekends, you might be unable to keep playing soccer or go camping with your friends. This is why it's so important to ask yourself: *What kind of life do I want to have?*

It makes sense to isolate your career when making decisions at school because it keeps it simple. People who have influenced you might not have all the information. They may not appreciate how vital other parts of your life are. You may not even understand them yet. It can lead to you making decisions early on that might not fit with how you want your life to be.

No one else is responsible for your career but you

In the introduction, I spoke about your career being a box you fill with work-related activities. A key difference between school and work is that *you* get to decide which activities you include in your career box. You are not at the mercy of the school your family chose or the teachers who taught your subject.

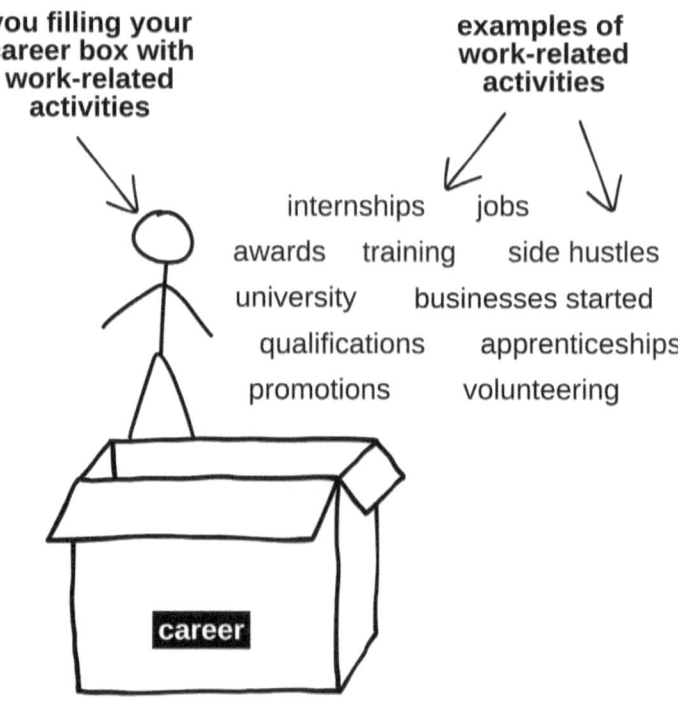

SCHOOL

Letting all the influences in your past dictate everything about your future isn't how you create an epic career. It took me ten years to fully understand that I was walking around feeling like a failure because I hadn't become a doctor. It felt like a massive weight off my shoulders when I finally owned it and embraced the path I was on instead.

So, it's time to draw a line in the sand. Are you going to sit back and watch your career from the sidelines—or jump into the game and become an active player in how it turns out?

Take ownership of your career, and it will take you on an incredible journey.

CHAPTER 2
THE CASUAL JOG YEARS

Like most twenty-one-year-olds, I found myself needing extra cash. While flicking through a local community newsletter, one job caught my eye:

> Silver polisher required for my private collection—will pay cash.

Thinking, 'How hard could it be?' I reached out by text to the lovely lady, who I assumed was called Gladys. Before I knew it, Gladys was calling me for an informal phone interview (I was so in).

When she asked if I had any experience polishing silver, I replied, 'Not specifically, but I back myself to get it done'. Apparently, that was an unacceptable answer. Gladys abruptly cut the phone call short, telling me she would only hire someone with experience. Rejected.

Let's start jogging

I briefly mentioned in the introduction that this book covers how to tackle the first five years of your career after school. I like to call this stage the *Casual Jog Years*. I'll explain why using this example:

> *I swore I would never be one of those people who just go for a run. It sounded like my idea of exercise torture. Then, one day last year, I unexpectedly had this bizarre urge to go for a run. I laced up my runners and hit the road, feeling like a hero. The next day, I laced up the runners again and went for another run. Same again on the third day. On the fourth day, I was in the physiotherapist's office with acupuncture needles poking into my ankles. I had damaged the tendons because I had jumped straight from walking into running, and my body went, 'WTF?'*

Up until this point in your career, you have been learning to walk, so to speak. A part-time job here, a traineeship application there. You assume that because you've mastered the walking stage, you're ready to go straight to running once school is over. Unfortunately, as I discussed in the last chapter, school probably hasn't nailed the task of preparing you for what's to come. It hasn't taught you how to run.

THE CASUAL JOG YEARS

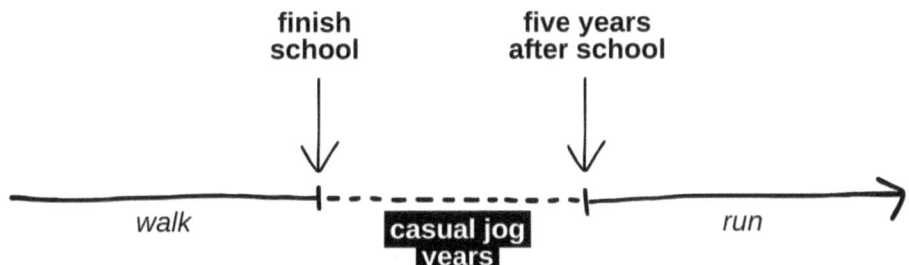

These five years after school can be a real hot mess. No one's forcing you to eat your vegetables daily, but you're old enough to know you should.

It's a stage in life where anything goes. You could have a friend with two kids by the age of twenty-two, another who has their own successful business by twenty-three, another who has switched university degrees three times but never finished any and another who has been to thirty countries and counting. Oh, and let's not forget, there's bound to be at least one friend living on their last $20.

But equally, there are wonderful opportunities to explore who you are and the world around you in a way you never could at school. Your experiences during this time are foundational to the person you become.

The way to make the most of these years is to treat them as a transition. They should be about taking some *casual jogs* while you build up the skills and strength to run (to clarify, you don't have to literally start jogging). A casual jog implies a more relaxed pace, maybe stopping to take in the sights along the way. There's a fluffy dog, so you stop to pat it. You aren't preoccupied with speed or trying to beat everyone. You are doing it to enjoy it.

What I'm suggesting is don't plan *forever*; give yourself these first five years of *whatever*. Assume what you want to do now is not what you'll actually be doing in ten years. Loose plans and ideas are excellent during this stage because they're flexible. You're stepping away from some of the influences we covered in the previous chapter and forging your own awesome path. Give yourself some breathing room.

All of the actions in this book are examples of taking a casual career jog. Nothing too heavy or strenuous, but certainly enough oomph to start moving. Keeping it light allows you to embrace the changes without becoming overwhelmed.

An example of The Casual Jog Years

Here is a snapshot of my first five years:
- Took a gap year overseas.
- Moved to Melbourne for university and lived on campus.
- Studied biomedical science in my first year.
- Moved home and worked my old job in a pharmacy for the summer.

- Added a commerce degree in my second year, majoring in finance (don't ask me what I was ever planning to do with that combination).
- Worked as a residential adviser (like a babysitter for university students).
- Moved in with my brother and started a full-time telemarketing job while studying.
- Dumped by another guy, but this time in the food court of a shopping centre.
- Studied abroad in the United States for a semester.

Here are five fun facts from the time between the end of my Casual Jog Years and now, some of which, I'll tell stories about later in the book:
- Moved to New Zealand when I was twenty-four and lived there for five years.
- Became a travel agent, slayed it, and then burned out.
- Learned how to snowboard.
- Bought a boat for $500.
- Took a second gap year and wrote this book.

Increase your career elasticity

I want to introduce a concept that can be helpful to focus on in your Casual Jog Years: creating and increasing your *career elasticity*.

Imagine a rubber band—the more elastic it is, the more you can stretch it in all directions without it breaking. You can think about your career in a similar way. You are going to face challenges. Opportunities that appear risky will be presented to you. You want to develop the career elasticity to bounce back from challenges and stretch yourself to take opportunities. The more you do this, the more resilient you become. You can face hardships with confidence.

When you overcome setbacks, you enhance your ability to deal with comparable or more significant obstacles. If you miss out on a job you wanted, you could complain and not move on from it. Or you can brush up on your interview game and try again. Working a weekend job to supplement your income while you complete an apprenticeship isn't ideal, but it builds a work ethic you can draw on later.

If you have been fortunate not to face too much adversity, there are creative ways to test yourself by completing *voluntary hardships*. Choose a task, select a length of time, and then dive in. It could be giving up for a period something you enjoy but isn't necessary for your survival (e.g. no streaming apps for a month). If you care about sustainability, you could challenge yourself not to purchase or consume anything packaged in single-use plastic. If you have a car and it's feasible, you could choose only to take public transport, walk or ride a bike. It doesn't matter if it seems silly as long as it challenges you.

Embracing opportunities is an equally important skill to master. This takes practice. It might feel scary to put your hand up to organise the staff Christmas party, but it could be a chance to show your leadership skills. Volunteering overseas for two weeks in your summer holidays might mean taking extra shifts to pay for it. But it might be the very thing that inspires you to become more financially secure so you can help those less fortunate.

A bonus lesson on time

If they haven't already, people will tell you life is short. What they mean, though, is that life goes fast. And if you don't chill out to soak it up, you are going to miss all the fun.

Do you remember being a child and Christmas felt like it took forrreeeevvvver to come around? Now, weeks and months seem to fly by? You can't even remember what you did last Tuesday, let alone three months ago.

Let me introduce a phenomenon called *time dilution*. As you get older, your relationship with time alters. A year when you're four feels longer than when you're eighteen. I'll use a pie chart to help explain it.

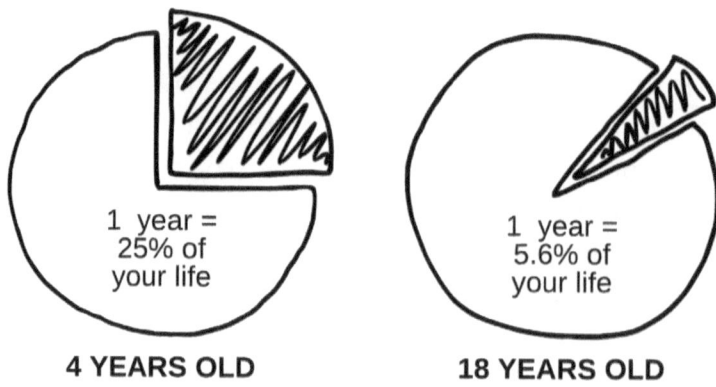

4 YEARS OLD   **18 YEARS OLD**

When you are four, one year is 25% of your life. Whereas when you are eighteen, one year is only 5.6% of your life.

Basically, each extra year you're on planet Earth feels shorter than the last. It leaves you with the sense that time is speeding up. There are two points I want to make based on this:
1. After school, years can easily pass you by if you're so focussed on getting to the next stage of your life (e.g. graduate university so you can start working in that field).
2. You are only at the beginning of your adult life. You have so much more to go. There is time available to chill.

CHAPTER 3
TAKE A GAP YEAR
(ACTION)

During my gap year after high school, I became a live-in nanny with a family in Italy for nine months. I was responsible for typical nanny tasks like getting the kids ready for school, handing out snacks and ensuring they didn't die before their parents came home. However, the main reason they hired me was so that their two sons could learn English. I figured that wouldn't be difficult since I'd been speaking English my whole life.

Wrong.

So. Very. Wrong.

One morning, about two months into the gig, the father came into the kitchen and said the six words no one wants to hear: 'We need to talk to you.' I was nineteen years old, on the other side of the world, about to be told I suck by a boss who I also lived with and would see at dinner.

I will never forget this rough line from the roasting that followed: 'The children's English is worse now than it was with their previous nanny.' How awful must I have been for a comment like that to be true?

Thankfully, I had another seven months to improve. While their English was slightly better when I left, I could tell the family was not sad to see me go. I did contribute some positive things to the household, though. My vanilla cupcakes were a hit.

—

If you follow only one action in your Casual Jog Years, please make it this one. I believe gap years should be compulsory for all school leavers—that's how passionate I am about them. I have yet to meet a person who has regretted taking a gap year, but I have met plenty who have regretted *not* taking one. It is single-handedly the best decision I made in my first five years, even if the nannying part didn't go to plan.

What is a gap year?

Traditionally, the term *gap year* refers to a period (usually twelve months) spent doing something other than studying between finishing high school and starting university.

TAKE A GAP YEAR

I suggest we apply the term gap year more generally to any period 'taken off' between finishing one phase of our lives and starting the next. For the purposes of this book, I'm referring to the period between school and the beginning of the next 'big thing'. That big thing might be university, starting an apprenticeship, committing to a longer-term job, etc.

This is how I like to picture gap years. Imagine this phase of your life as a sandwich. School is one piece of bread, and the next big thing is the other piece of bread. You don't have an exciting sandwich if you only slap the two pieces of bread together. A gap year is the tasty filling or spread that joins the two slices. You use a gap year to glue together the two phases of your life.

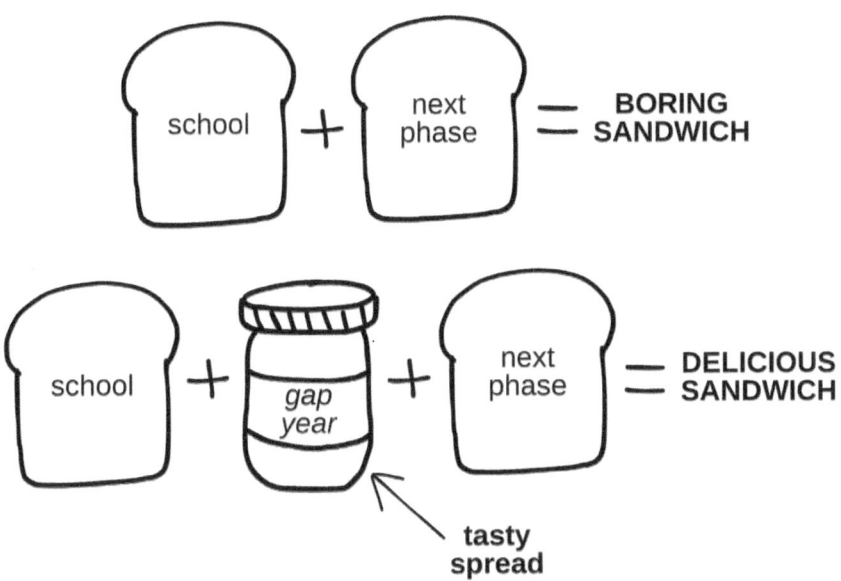

Reasons to take a gap year

Gap years are all about *opportunity*. What do you want to do? Who do you want to meet? How much money do you want to make? Anything is possible in a gap year because you're not restrained by school or someone else telling you what to do.

Let's look at four reasons why taking a gap year might be a smart idea:

Rest
School and study have dominated your schedule for the past thirteen years (give or take). Add a social life, part-time jobs, hobbies or sports, and you have put in an impressive effort. You deserve a break.

Assess
A gap year takes the pressure off making too many career decisions straight out of school. You can weigh up your options without committing to a particular pathway.

Explore
This is a fantastic time to gain life and career experience outside your education. Savour some freedom, work in an industry you're attracted to, volunteer, travel. There are unlimited options.

Prepare
You can earn and save money. You can mentally and emotionally prepare for the next stage. You can pick up a new skill or focus on making connections.

My gap year was about resting and exploring. The idea of being a nanny in Italy came from wanting to speak Italian fluently (and a general obsession with pizza).

What you can get up to on a gap year

The table below provides examples of how all or part of a gap year could be filled.

Work	Activities	Travel	Learning
Work and live at home.	Discover a new hobby.	Travel interstate.	Complete a pre-apprenticeship course.
Internship at a company in an industry you're keen to work in.	Train for a marathon.	Apply for a working holiday visa, move overseas and work in a foreign country.	Volunteer for a cause you care about.
Join the military for a year (if that's an option in your country.)	Become an amateur skateboarder. Take art classes for fun.	Take a road trip with your friends.	Enrol in an online course that gives you a skill that people will pay you for.
Turn an interest like photography into a side hustle.		Spend summer working in a beachy tourist town.	Learn how to code.

How to plan a gap year

There is no perfect way to plan a gap year. However, a loose plan is better than winging it for twelve months. You don't need to have every detail planned out before the year begins, and you can always make adjustments. I'm going to start you off.

1. Dream a little

There's no such thing as a terrible idea for your gap year. Generate some loose plans about what you could do and how you might do it. Use your imagination and a little creativity. Nannying in Italy was a pipedream until I researched how to do it. If you've never had a job, find one and gain some experience. It doesn't matter where it is or if you quit after three months.

The following are questions to help the creative juices flow:
- *What would you love to do?*
  Having one initial focus, goal, or activity is helpful. Focus on fitness. Save $20,000. Play one song on a guitar.
- *How could you break up the year?*
  Work for six months to save, travel for three months, then work for another three months.
- *What could you do for work?*
  Stay at a current part-time job and search for something else to add alongside it.
- *Where would you live?*
  At home. With a friend or cousin. Overseas.

- *How could you fund this year?*
  Savings. Working. Loan from family.
- *Who would you love to spend some of your gap year with, and what could you do together?*
  Go snorkelling in Thailand with a partner. Build a dirt bike track with a friend.

It can also be worth considering what is available in your local area and what would require less effort to organise. That's not to say you should be lazy about planning a gap year; you just don't have to make it more complicated than it needs to be. An easy-to-organise, simple gap year can be as punchy as any.

2. Research
Once you have generated some ideas, start researching and gathering information. This is how you can eliminate options and make progress toward others.

You wouldn't be the first person to take a gap year, so there will be plenty of advice out there from people who have likely already done something similar to what you are contemplating. Listen to podcasts. Ask your boss about options for full-time employment. Start putting a budget together for any travel plans.

3. Make some decisions
Once you feel confident to start locking in some of your plans, commit by taking at least one step. It could be

applying to defer your university course or creating a savings tracker to hang up on your wall. It doesn't have to be anything huge; simply a step that says to yourself *I'm doing this.*

Common myths and concerns

You might be nervous about taking a gap year or feel it's not an option. This section will address some concerns and debunk a few myths.

Parents
Your parents might be worried that you won't go to university or do anything productive with your life if you take a gap year. It's as if they assume you'll sit in your bedroom for twelve hours daily and play video games—ironic because the gaming industry is enormous and a viable career pathway.

My point is that parents have a habit of thinking in worst-case scenarios and can sometimes miss the possible upsides. They also have their own ideas about what's best for your career (which are often based on their own experiences—good and bad). The landscape has dramatically changed since they were in your position, and what matters has shifted. The average retirement age has been pushed back, meaning you might spend longer in the workforce than they do. A year at the beginning to focus on something you enjoy or that builds some savings doesn't harm your long-term prospects.

If you're nervous about how your parents will react to you taking a gap year (or you need their support), start with a gentle, open conversation. Pick a time when they're not tired, hungry or working. If you have already put a potential plan together, you might be able to use this to show your level of commitment. It will hopefully be the first of many productive conversations.

University
University is a massive time, energy, and financial commitment. I have heard the reasons why you might not take a gap year before starting a degree. These are some classics, and my responses:
- *If I don't go now, I'll never go.* It's not the end of the world if you don't.
- *I'll be behind.* Behind what, behind who? If anything, you'll be ahead in life experience, which counts for A LOT.
- *It will take me ages to graduate, so I should start and get it over and done with.* And burn out because all you have done is study? You'll be a far better university student for taking a gap year.

Taking a break lets you properly analyse your options and clear your head *before* getting caught up in university's excitement and study commitments. Shouldn't you go to university because you want to be there instead of forcing yourself and regretting the student loan later?

Graduating within three years of leaving school does not make you stand out. Spending a year doing something totally different does.

An alternative might be to complete the first year of a degree and then take a gap year. The structure of university is much more flexible than high school. It is normal to be in the same class as someone two years ahead, one year behind or five years older than you.

Other potential concerns

> *Gap years do not have to cost much money, nor are they only for people from rich families.*
> As I've already covered, you can choose to work during this time. You could earn money for part of the year and volunteer the rest. The options are endless, and they don't all require money upfront.
>
> *You don't have to travel in your gap year or live overseas.*
> I knew travel was something I wanted to do, but I know others who had no desire to do so. Both of my brothers took gap years and were employed full-time.
>
> *A gap year does not have to be one whole year.*
> Maybe you want to start an apprenticeship halfway

through the year. You can take a gap half-year. A friend of mine even took two gap years one after another, working at an American summer camp the first and a British school boarding house the other.

Just because none of your friends are doing it doesn't mean you can't.
It can be tempting to follow what everyone else is doing, but if there's something you know you want to do, trust that.

You do not have to take a gap year immediately after school.
I recommend this only because it is when you can arguably gain the most benefit. If there is a legitimate reason that you can't or shouldn't postpone (for example, a scholarship), you can always take one later.

Funding a gap year

Before I lived in Italy as a nanny, I spent three months travelling solo in North America and Europe. I stayed in hostels. Half of my meals were peanut butter on bread. I caught the 5am flight if it saved $15. It wasn't fancy, but it was epic.

I funded the entire gap year myself with savings from part-time jobs I had at school and the small allowance I earned while nannying. On average, my allowance was equivalent to $110 a week and the Italian family covered my living costs (shelter, food, transport). However, I also had the financial safety net of my parents. I knew I could fly back to Australia with nothing left in my bank account and stay with them before I started university. Ultimately, this did happen, and I spent the summer working full-time at my old job to get back on my feet. I know how fortunate I am to have had this support; your situation may differ from this. I don't want this to discourage you from taking a gap year. There are multiple ways to make a gap year happen. Find one that works for you.

Me: *Customers are the WORST.*
Customer: *I'm standing right here.*
Me: *They ALWAYS ruin my day.*
Customer: *Can you see me?*
Me: *Work would be SO much better if I didn't have to deal with them.*
Customer: *Do you want my money or not?*
Me: *I don't see why I should have to serve them.*
Customer: *Fine, I'll take my money elsewhere!*

—

Me: *Gosh, that customer was rude.*

CHAPTER 4
THE BASIC CAREER PRINCIPLES

At twenty-five and well into my what-the-fuck-am-I-doing-with-my-life-phase, I moved to New Zealand with my boyfriend. I wanted to do something I was good at (sales) within an area I was passionate about (travel). I became a travel agent and thrived. There was a work hard, play hard culture, and I did both.

I qualified to attend the company's international conference for the top achievers in Las Vegas. All expenses paid. It was a crazy high in my career. What I didn't realise at the time was that I was about to go through my biggest low within a matter of months.

My downfall was taking a promotion. I wasn't ready to lead a sales team. There were days when I would drive to the office while it was still dark outside, with tears streaming down my face. There were nights when I would still be in the office at 10pm. I was empty, ruined and burnt out. I had lost all my passion for travel and sales. I was living a life I hadn't signed up for. My career had somehow become way too serious.

—

This chapter will cover three basic principles at the core of the Unserious Careers approach.

Principle 1: One career, many jobs

Your career is effectively formed by the series of decisions you make. Turn down that job offer, accept this one, move across the country, go back to study, suck in that interview, take time off to travel etc.

Nothing you do in your career is a waste of time because every single thing you do builds on everything before it. You never have to 'start over' again in a *different* career. You cannot go backward because you are forever contributing to one career. Even though you might be applying for an entry-level position to establish yourself in a new industry, you bring all your previous experiences. No door is ever truly closed because all you ever are is a decision away from your next amazing opportunity. Knowing this allows you to jump at unexpected opportunities along the way.

The danger of a 'dream job'

If I asked you what your dream job is—what would it be? Is it one of those fantasy dream jobs you'd likely never actually do? Or is it one that you'd actively put the time into?

I ask these questions because there is a danger in labelling something as a 'dream job'. You might be setting yourself up for disappointment. Why? Those dream roles are often only a dream because they sound promising on paper. But the day-to-day reality is rarely so glamorous.

Compare it to dating: if you asked me at eighteen who my dream partner was, I probably would have said Ryan Gosling. But let's be honest; I would have been basing that answer on how attractive I found him and how much money he made. Not what it would have *felt* like to date him. Maybe he's as dull as a doorknob to talk to?

Instead, I highly recommend making a list of jobs or work opportunities you would love to try. This will become your career bucket list.

Be as ridiculous as you want with these. It was absurd that I would win trips overseas as a travel agent—until I did and ticked it off my career bucket list. It doesn't have to be specific jobs. It could be something such as working in a giant factory. It could be working with a mate or making $1 million in a year. Nothing is too ridiculous to be on your list.

What you do for work is only one aspect of your life (remember that diagram from Chapter 1?). Don't hold out for your dream job to start enjoying the rest of it.

Principle 2: Experiment first, commit later

What I essentially mean by this principle is: try before you buy. However, *experimenting* sounds way more thrilling than *trying*. Trying feels like what I do with my dirty clothes: I try to put them straight in the washing basket, but they mostly end up on the floor. When you experiment, you're in. You're doing it. You're taking ownership. Experimenting is the only thing that can give you an authentic taste of the ideas you receive from others and online. It allows you to collect data and make better decisions throughout your career.

It's a process of elimination

Through experimenting, I am encouraging you to go through a process of elimination. Sometimes, the most effective way to determine what you *do* want is to find out what you *don't* want. You might have a terrible boss who micromanages you, and you decide to avoid anyone like that in the future. You might try the night shift and know it's not for you, so you only look for options with daytime hours.

If you do enough experimenting (and therefore eliminating), my theory is that you will eventually land on something you do want. I spent most of my twenties having no idea what I really wanted. But I experimented enough that finally, I reached a tipping point where I knew enough about what I didn't want that I could instead begin tapping into what I did want.

But how do you know what to experiment with?

Being told to experiment in your first five years might feel like being told to bake a cake—in a kitchen you've never used—in a house you've never been to—when the recipe is written in hieroglyphics.

The actions in this book will give you some ideas about experimenting with your career. However, in the Casual Jog Years, you might be keen to experiment in areas outside work such as:
- **Lifestyle** – living by the beach, working weekends.
- **Education** – online learning, on-the-job training.
- **Social life** – pick up a new hobby, make new friends.
- **Health** – join a gym, see a therapist.

Experimenting doesn't need to cost money. You don't have to embark on some grand adventure or sign a long-term contract at a company to experiment effectively. You can experiment with the tiniest of things, such as what it would be like to eat dinner for breakfast and breakfast for dinner. Small changes can still teach you plenty about yourself, the world and what you want from your career.

Of course, some experiments can make money if we're referring to employment or starting your own business. In my early twenties, I signed up to participate in a sleep study with my university. They paid me $150 to track my sleep for two weeks. Being paid to sleep was a neat experiment. Another example is when I took a job as a business manager for a real estate team. I had always thought I would get a kick out of being a real estate agent. It was a way to sample the industry without committing too deeply. By the end of the first week, I knew I was happy where I was and that I didn't want to sell houses.

Unpaid internships and volunteering are brilliant to explore. These types of work tend to be a long-term gain. You do the unpaid work now to build the knowledge and connections for a role in the future. Doing the unpaid summer internship could confirm what you are studying is exactly what you want to do. However, time spent on these activities is time that you can't make money to pay your current bills. You don't want to be taken advantage of, so ensure you can still look after yourself while pursuing them.

Sunk cost fallacy

There is a trap that you should keep an eye out for in these years: the sunk cost fallacy. It is when you continue doing something because you have already committed (i.e., sunk) so much time or money into it, even though you know it would be equally beneficial to stop. You feel like if you quit, all the time and money would have been for nothing. It could mean continuing an apprenticeship because you don't want to lose the two years you've already spent doing it. It could look like staying at university studying in a field you're confident you'll never work within because you don't want to waste what you've already completed.

Experimenting is how you can prevent falling into this trap. It could be completing a pre-apprenticeship course before the apprenticeship to make sure it feels right. It could be labouring on a construction site before approaching your boss about becoming a builder. It could be working as a receptionist in a law firm to suss out the industry before starting your law degree.

If you find yourself partway through something you're no longer into, know it is an option to stop and do something else. As we covered in the first principle—nothing you do in your career is a waste of time. You will still have the skills and connections you gained from those experiences you can take with you. If the ship is sinking, get off as early as possible before it takes you down with it.

Principle 3: You matter most; look after yourself

The thing you never want to do in these years is settle—settle for a shit job working for a nasty boss while dating a loser and hanging out with friends you don't even like on the weekend. It's ok to be a quitter in these years because it's far better than settling for situations that make you miserable. This is the time to be selfish and put yourself first. You can be selfish and prioritise yourself without being a jerk.

If your job situation isn't panning out—be ready to move on sooner rather than later before your mental and physical health suffers. You might not be financially able to hand in your notice tomorrow without another gig secured. If that is the case, put a plan in place so you know the actions you need to take before quitting.

Bosses might try to guilt you when you leave, but you don't owe them anything beyond doing your job until the end of your last shift. If I have a great relationship with my boss, I might consider giving an extra week or two notice that I'm quitting. But if I am worried they will take my leaving badly, I'll only do what's legally required. You don't have to be loyal to an employer because they took a chance on you. Remember, they hired you because it was in *their* best interest, not yours.

—

THE BASIC CAREER PRINCIPLES

Shortly after the Las Vegas high, I unexpectedly quit my travel agent job. My boss was rattled. The company had placed a lot of faith in me to make them proud (and make them a ton of money). I felt sick the day I handed in my resignation. I knew I would be letting them down. But dammit, I was done with letting myself down.

—

I said it in the introduction, but it's worth repeating—taking the Unserious Careers approach means that work should add awesome into your life, not take the fun away. This is crucial to your long-term well-being.

You can still do work that has serious consequences. Hey, someone needs to perform heart surgery and enforce the law. It simply means you do it because you want to, not because someone thinks you should. These jobs, even if they are more serious in nature, should still allow you to live a satisfying life.

When your career feels it is getting too serious, come back to something unserious. For me, that means doing something fun that makes me laugh, like watching stand-up comedy. For you, that could be building an obstacle course for your pet guinea pig, Gary.

Be ready for new opportunities; sometimes, they come sooner than you expected and require you to reach out and take them. You don't owe anyone anything. Always have your bags packed.

CHAPTER 5
QUALIFICATIONS

WHAT'S A PIECE OF PAPER WORTH?

Tom is charismatic AF. He is the kind of guy who will make an awful joke but still make you laugh because of how happy it made him. Tom chose to take a gap year and defer the offer he received to study journalism. He worked in hospitality before heading to Queenstown, New Zealand, for a skiing trip. Queenstown is known as a party and adventure capital, so it was a dream for a kid without a care in the world. He was hooked and cancelled his flight home, saying thanks but no thanks to his university offer.

Within days, he found a job at a bungee jumping company. He went from working in the cafe to spending his days on the bungee ledge, preparing people for their jump before waving them goodbye.

Tom stayed with the same company for seven years.

An opportunity then presented itself at a rival tourism operator in their management trainee program. He jumped at it (pun intended). He has now worked at different sites in New Zealand, Singapore and Canada. In less than two years, he became an operations manager—at twenty-six years old and with no university degree behind him.

What are your qualifications?

Writing a chapter on qualifications for this book felt like swallowing dry toast while dehydrated—unpleasant, messy and frankly dangerous. The post-school education and training industry is a behemoth. In these five years, everyone is fighting for your money or your labour. I was scared to piss off the wrong person by dissing one option or favouring another. But qualifications are vital to the career conversation, so let's talk.

The first examples of qualifications that pop into your head might be 'formal' or 'official', such as a bachelor's degree or an apprenticeship. However, they come in all shapes and sizes. Basically, a qualification means you have skills, knowledge or experience that make you suitable for a particular position, workplace or task. It indicates you have accomplished *this*, so now you can do *that*.

Some qualifications are mandatory for a profession (i.e., to work as an optometrist or an electrician). Some will help you earn more money. Some will not give you a certificate at the end but are more attractive to an employer than a PhD. This chapter will hopefully shed the light you need to make clearer decisions for the future.

How to use qualifications effectively

If you use Google Maps to direct you to a friend's house, the app will give you multiple transport options. Qualifications operate similarly in your career: they are like modes of transport you can choose between to take you where you want to go. You use them to move from point A to point B in your career (and to points C, D, E and beyond).

Here are four general qualification modes:

> *University—like taking a train.*
> It will rarely get you exactly where you need to be, but it can be a direct and efficient route to a general area. A teaching job requires an education degree, but even then, some leg work is necessary to be hired.
>
> *Apprenticeships—like driving a car.*
> You need to be confident in the direction, or you will end up on the opposite side of the city. You're in control, making the turns and watching out for hazards.
>
> *Micro-credentials—like riding a bike.*

Micro-credentials, for the sake of this book, refer to any qualification that takes less than twelve months to complete. These are short and effective ways to jump between one place and another without too much sweat. Easy to pick up and put down.

On-the-job experience—like walking.
You're nimble and can explore anywhere, reaching destinations no other mode can. It will take longer to reach faraway places initially, but if where you're going is right around the corner, why would you catch a train, drive or ride there?

The mode you choose will influence your experience of the journey between points A and B. It will determine *what, how* and *where* you will learn. It will decide *who* you learn from and *when* you become qualified.

With this in mind, there are some ground rules you might want to consider when choosing between qualifications:
- No mode is superior to another (provided it isn't a job needing a specific qualification). It comes down to how you want to learn during this period.
- You likely will use a combination of two or more in your career. If you desperately want to be a rocket tester (that has to be an official job title, right?), I doubt NASA will let you play with billion-dollar toys the first day after graduating from aerospace engineering.

QUALIFICATIONS

- Even within the same qualification mode, there can be many ways to complete it (e.g. online, in-person, hybrid).

—

Michael started an apprenticeship in greenkeeping (working on a golf course) when he was twenty-nine. He loved the sport and being outdoors. After school, Michael studied pharmacy for a year but decided there was too much chemistry, so switched to a psychology degree. He graduated but has never worked a day in the field. Yet, he has been able to apply what he learned to every single workplace since. Most people are confused by a greenkeeper who also studied psychology, but it's precisely what makes him such a valuable employee.

Comparing the modes

The table below broadly compares how costly the modes are in terms of dollars and time.

	University	Apprenticeship	Micro-credential	On-the-job experience
Cost	Very high (e.g. $20k+).	No cost - paid to learn.	Low to medium (e.g. $100-$10k).	No cost - paid to gain experience.
Time	Three years or more; part or full-time.	Two years or more; generally full-time.	One year or less; it could be completed in a few hours.	Varies; anything from weeks to years.

1. *University*

I want to acknowledge that university may not have been presented as an option to you at school because you weren't 'smart enough'. Or it might be financially out of reach. I don't want you to read this and think about how it must be nice for people with academic or financial abilities to attend university. There are many pathways into university if it is something you genuinely want to do, and many also offer micro-credentials. Because of how misrepresented it can be, I will do an extra dive into university at the end of this chapter.

Benefits
- They're a widely recognised qualification that may help you leapfrog into a job you wouldn't otherwise be able to apply for.
- It's a potentially smoother transition between school and full-time work.
- You have the option to switch between degrees (as long as you have the prerequisites) and receive some credit for studies you have already completed.

Limitations
- It's a significant cost and commitment—if you quit a degree halfway through, the university unfortunately doesn't give you a certificate saying you're 50% architect.
- You can be taught outdated concepts and might lack practical skills upon completion.
- Often, there's no clear pathway once you graduate

from general or broad degrees.

2. Apprenticeships and traineeships

While you will have heard of popular apprenticeships such as electrical, plumbing, building and hairdressing, there are hundreds more that you might not be familiar with. A cabinet maker's different from a carpenter, who is different from a joiner. There are chefs, pastry chefs and bakers. You can become a diesel mechanic, light vehicle mechanic, marine mechanic or refrigeration mechanic. There's glazing, tiling and bricklaying. A metal fabricator is not the same as a boilermaker. You can do a landscaping or sports turf apprenticeship, but you can also do a horticulture traineeship. How about a butcher or a barber? A childcare, dental assistant or legal administration trainee. Let's stop there before your brain explodes from all the possibilities.

Benefits
- You are paid to learn by your employer and don't accrue student debt.
- From day one, you're gaining practical, hands-on experience which means less theory and more doing.
- Once fully qualified, many self-employment opportunities exist (e.g., subcontracting, starting a business and hiring your own apprentice).

Limitations
- The schedule is not very flexible—it's often a full-time commitment.

- Generally, you have to start over again if you switch from one apprenticeship to another (e.g. building to plumbing).
- You can feel trapped within the trade, i.e. there might be limited options to 'move up' in the company or industry, especially if it is a small or family-run business.

3. Micro-credentials

Given the shorter timeframe to earn them, micro-credentials are especially great for anyone with a fear of commitment. Examples could be anything from gaining a forklift licence after a two-day course to becoming a police officer after six months of academy training. It could be undertaking a self-paced online program to be a makeup artist, personal trainer or yoga instructor.

Benefits
- The cost tends to be a fraction of a bachelor's degree.
- They are a great way to experiment without locking into an extended qualification.
- They can be used to upskill within a job.

Limitations
- The fees might need to be paid upfront.
- You can only gain so much expertise, and the micro-credential alone may not be enough to qualify you for a specific job.
- Depending on the provider, the quality can vary wildly.

Watch out for dodgy companies that might make false claims, such as their qualifications being 'industry-recognised'. Upon further research, you might discover that they're really serving you the qualification equivalent of dog food but calling it steak.

4. On-the-job or life experience

Remember Tom from the start of this chapter? He has forged almost his entire career through on-the-job experience. You don't technically need any officially recognised qualification to build a satisfying career. Within the same company, you could start as a retail sales assistant in a shopping centre. You could be promoted to assistant store manager, store manager, then regional manager. After this, you might use all this experience and switch to the human resources department at the head office.

Benefits
- Flexible—there are many avenues, and you can pivot or pause whenever you like.
- You earn money as you qualify.
- Receive real work experience from day one to leverage for future moves.

Limitations
- Need to be self-led—there's no clear path set out in the first five years.
- You can get 'stuck' in the first thing you fall into, especially if you're not exposed to anyone outside

your industry.
- It can be tougher to get going—you may need to start right at the bottom of a company.

On-the-job experience is a *sticky* qualification: it sticks brilliantly to every other qualification mode. It says, 'I walked the talk', even if you don't have a flash piece of paper from an external source to show. It's all about how you communicate your experience or how creative you can get with applying it to new situations. All roads lead to this qualification mode sooner or later.

—

University: full disclosure

$56,037.15

This is the amount of money I currently owe the Australian government for my university education. I am starting this section with this figure because for any young person who does not have a scholarship or parents paying tuition, studying at university will mean accruing debt.

If you're struggling to comprehend whether $56,037.15 is a lot of money, ask yourself when the last time was that you tried to save $5,000. Seems like effort, right? Now multiply that effort by ten. We should also add that your tuition is only *one* cost associated with university. If you're like me and have to relocate to attend, there will be other living expenses.

I don't want you to fear university and not go because it costs money. I'm not anti-university. But I am a fan of giving you the knowledge you need to make an informed choice, and if you choose to go, how you can make the most of it.

I want to emphasise that I'm only talking about university for these first five years. The choice to go or what to study changes the older you become because your responsibilities shift, e.g. you have a mortgage, kids, or you've adopted seven stray cats.

Marketing tactics

I'm going to tell you a story that I will then use to explain the marketing tactics universities use.

> *In primary school, each student in my class submitted a poem they wrote into a nationwide poetry competition. Mine was about dairy farms. A couple of months passed, and I received a letter in the mail at home to congratulate me. My poem had been specially selected to feature in a printed edition of poems from the competition! All my parents had to do to accept this offer was purchase a copy of the book. 'Of course, what an honour!' they said. When the eight-hundred-page poetry book arrived, it became*

clear that every participant was 'specially selected' to feature. It was only the suckers who paid that had their poems included.

A university will make all these fancy-sounding claims:
- *All our students are treated as individuals.*
- *According to industry reports, our degrees are recognised in the top 11% by employers.*
- *We've been ranked 43rd in the world for the best universities to study at.*

They'll talk about how studies show people with bachelor degrees earn 23%* more on average than people without. And how 93%* of their graduates are employed full-time within twelve months of graduating. Blah, blah, blah. (*I'm making these figures up but you hopefully get the general idea.)

So, you apply for a degree at the university. If you have the prerequisites and make the cut, they say, 'Congratulations! You're in.' You're thrilled; what an accomplishment to receive a place. You accept their offer, enrol as a student and sign a few forms. You ask the government to pay the university on your behalf and agree that there is now an I-O-U to pay the government back. (The student loan system may differ depending on the country you're in.)

You turn up to your first lecture or log in to your first online class, look around the room and see 327 other students studying the same degree as you. *What was all that talk about treating students as individuals?*

Universities, at the end of the day, are businesses. You are a paying customer. They create scarcity, i.e. 'not everyone gets in', and we catch university FOMO—*LET ME IN!*

The debt is presented as an investment in your future. Which it can be. But here is the thing. Completing a degree at a university provides no guarantee of employment. There is no guarantee that because you completed a Bachelor of Finance, you can obtain a job in finance. There is no guarantee that you will even have the practical skills to apply for one. I use the finance example because I majored in finance through my commerce degree and graduated with almost no workplace-specific skills.

What's good about university

There is something I wish had been drilled into me from day one:

University is about the experience, not the qualification.

Using the description from earlier, university is about the journey between points A and B, not about everything that happens when you get to B. By only doing the bare minimum required to earn your degree; you are doing yourself a massive disservice. University is DIFFERENT to high school and how you approach it should reflect this. Too many people treat university as a continuation of school and wait to be told what to do rather than taking ownership of their experience.

The university environment can offer rich experiences that are difficult to find elsewhere. You can meet interesting people who, like you, are figuring out how to be adults. It is an incredibly vibrant atmosphere on campus. There are clubs, societies, sporting teams and performance groups to be involved in. Sticking behind for a few minutes after a lesson ends to chat to a professor or fellow student might open doors you didn't know were available. Be sure to keep this in mind if you are weighing up studying online vs on campus.

Hot tips for university

If you have taken a train in a city before, you might be familiar with express trains. These trains skip certain stops on a line to transit faster between one central train station and another. Many people treat university the same. They jump on the university express train and ride it straight to graduation.

QUALIFICATIONS

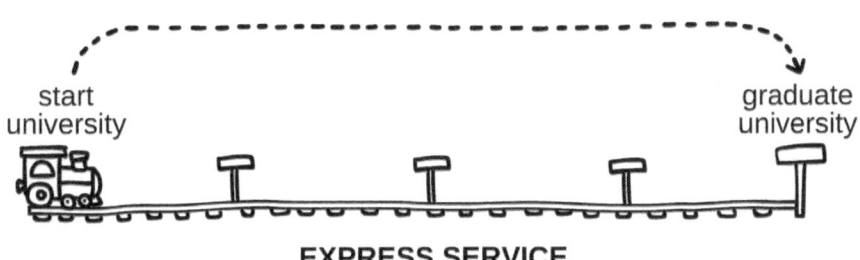

EXPRESS SERVICE

Instead, you should treat university as the train that stops at all stations. You don't have to hop off at each stop but give yourself the option to explore. While this might extend your travel time, it enhances your journey. You also give yourself the option to not continue until graduation if university is not for you or skip across to another qualification mode.

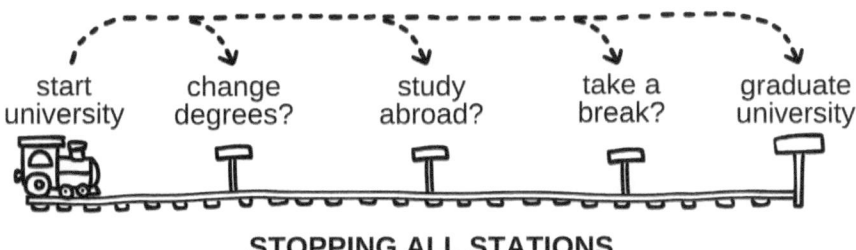

STOPPING ALL STATIONS

With this in mind, here are some tips:
- Research your options and weigh the costs. How much would that degree cost you? What would your employment prospects be?
- Talk to your parents or family. Ask what kind of financial support, if any, they could provide you with.

Consider living on campus if this option is financially available to you for the first year. It can be a great way to transition into university and make friends.
- If you're keen to explore what it's like to live in another country—studying abroad is a brilliant way to do it. Touch base with the study abroad team to see what would be required (often, you need a minimum grade average).
- You can quit university if you start and decide it isn't for you. It has not been a waste of time. A bigger waste of time is staying then regretting the additional debt (this is the sunk cost fallacy from Chapter 4 in action).
- Universities often have a resource hub for summer internships and graduate programs. Utilise these to connect the dots between the lecture theatre and the workplace.

CHAPTER 6
QUIT AT LEAST TWO PAID JOBS
(ACTION)

In his gap year, my brother Chris found employment at a slaughterhouse. Yes, a place where sheep went in on their own four legs and came out in boxes. Apologies for the mental image, but at least we're on the same page.

On his first shift, he was told to stand in one spot for eight hours and clean the butts of hundreds of lambs using a high-pressure hose. He lasted two shifts. It wasn't the physical component that disagreed with him. No, it was the nature of the business that he didn't vibe with. What he witnessed at the slaughterhouse in those two shifts mildly traumatised him.

Jobs in your Casual Jog Years

In these years, I encourage you to soak up as much as possible in every job, even if it's not what you want to do forever.

This action is Quit At Least Two Paid Jobs because:
- Working in two or more jobs means you can compare and contrast your experiences to make meaningful conclusions about what you do and do not like.
- Quitting isn't always easy. You must choose to walk away, knowing you might be letting someone down or giving up future opportunities. Quitting two or more jobs means you can practise what can be a brutal process when the stakes are potentially lower.

Remember, at this point, you are exploring what else is out there. You don't want to become too attached to a job during this time. Otherwise, you might find yourself ten years down the track at a company you no longer align with but are too scared to leave. Quitting is character-building and awesome for your career elasticity. You also collect skills from working through the job cycle multiple times.

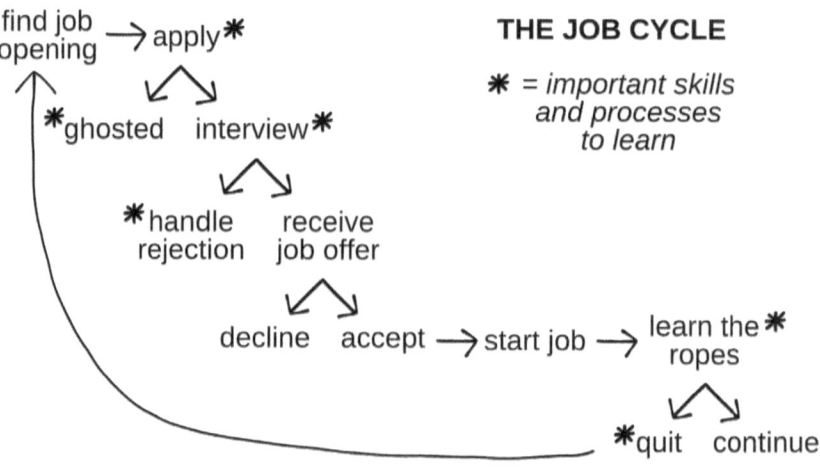

Below are four general tips about the jobs you apply for during this time. These aren't tips on landing them but how to decide which ones to look for.

All jobs are equal.
During this time, no job is superior to another. No job is a waste of time, regardless of how terrible you think it is. You can learn as much from bartending as interning at a marketing agency. Crappy and boring ones are great too. You will be shocked by how much these teach you about what you don't want. You might find that a low-effort job allows you to save energy for other important activities in your life.

Be paid for your time.
These jobs should ideally pay you instead of a non-paying position such as volunteering or unpaid internships. While these are valuable, I believe you also need exposure to more than one job with something financially on the line.

Respect your limitations.
As much as we try to pretend otherwise—money matters. While I suggest you experiment with different jobs, you must ensure you can pay the bills and not be on the brink of a financial meltdown. If you have study commitments, be mindful of what you can take on. Don't forget your social life, either.

Set yourself up with the right expectations.
Your life isn't over if the new job doesn't go to plan. If you're placing unrealistic expectations on it, you might be disappointed if it doesn't go the way you were really, really, really hoping it would. It's ok to be terrible at a job you thought you would excel at. Or hate a job you thought could be 'the one'.

Timing is everything.
You *can* do everything you want, just not all at once. You might have a list of ten jobs you want to try, but you don't have to chase them all at once. The age at which you do a job can make a sizable difference in whether you enjoy it. When you're nineteen, you might prefer something with more action and colleagues of a similar age.

More jobs are better than one

If you saw my resume at the end of those first five years, it was a bizarre combination: nanny, pharmacy assistant, residential adviser, telemarketer, receptionist and food delivery driver. And yet, I could talk for hours about what each of them taught me.

The amount that you learn from doing a variety of jobs is astronomical. At this stage, most of what you know is directly related to school/family/friends. We want to broaden these horizons.

QUIT AT LEAST TWO PAID JOBS

In some ways, you would be better off having five different jobs in these five years than one job for five years. Contemplate how much knowledge you could gather from five separate workplaces and bosses with their own quirks. Not to mention the exposure you might receive across industries.

There is no minimum amount of time you need to spend in a role. If it sucks after two weeks and you can't gain anything further from it, quit. If the workplace is toxic and you can feel it impacting your mental health, quit. You might need another job lined up if you don't have the money or financial assistance to pay your bills while you look. But as I've said previously—you don't owe an employer anything in these years. You matter most.

Let me address one of the biggest concerns you (or the people in your life who care about you) might have about not staying in jobs for a long time. That is, how potential future employers might interpret it.

Firstly, I want to reiterate that this book is not a career strategy for life; it is an approach for the first five years after school, i.e., the Casual Jog Years. I'm not suggesting you move jobs every six months for the next fifteen years. Chill.

Secondly, the job market has changed, especially with the rise of freelancing and the gig economy. Working for decades at the same company is so pre-2010. If someone has issues with you experimenting in these five years and expects you to stay in one spot, this might be a red flag. You don't want to work for someone with outdated ideas of what makes a terrific young candidate.

Thirdly, you can use the variety of jobs to stand out. Maybe it shows to an employer you're a go-getter and bringing varied experience to a role you want to settle into.

Some skills you pick up might not make sense at the time, but they can be useful in the long run. Driving traffic from a social media account to a website might not make much sense if you're studying to be a nuclear physicist at the same time. But what if, five years down the road, you decide to start a physics podcast and it becomes a raging success? To monetise you might consider selling merchandise from a website. I bet you'd be glad you had that social media experience from a part-time job.

Help if you're stuck for ideas

While all jobs are equal during this time, I don't want to leave you directionless. Jobs that help you get ridiculously *people-smart* early in your career can be highly advantageous.

Being people-smart means having the ability to understand and effectively communicate with a wide variety of people. You know how to listen and ask amazing questions. You are emotionally intelligent and have empathy for others. These are some of the most sought-after qualities in the workplace. They're not something you have to be born with; you can develop them over time.

The key to boosting your people-smarts is networking and interacting with as many people from different walks of life as possible—different ages, nationalities and demographics. Customer service jobs are brilliant for this, as are sales roles.

Customer service
I'm always suspicious if someone says their first part-time job was good. Every person's first job should involve being nervous that someone from school might see you working. In my case, that involved wearing a white hair net and a bright orange apron. This combination did no favours for my teenage acne. I sliced deli meats, roasted chickens and served customers for $7.62 an hour at the local supermarket. I also perfected the art of mysteriously disappearing to the cool room anytime I saw someone I knew coming my way.

—

Customer service could be anything from waiting tables to crushing it at the checkout of a department store, as long as it involves you directly connecting with the public.

The people skills you acquire in these roles are second to none. The jobs are generally super dynamic, meaning you must problem-solve on the fly. You will be interacting as a customer with people in roles like hospitality and retail for the rest of your life. After you have been in their shoes and seen the worst of society, you have a new level of appreciation for what they do. You become kinder and more patient, especially with the poor person serving customers on Christmas Eve.

Sales
I had doubts about taking a job as a telemarketer, but I was a university student, the money was decent, and my hours would be flexible. Sure, I was verbally abused over the phone at least twice a day, but it required minimal mental effort. Essentially, all I had to do was read the same script one hundred times a day.

The highly repetitive role meant the staff didn't last long. Or they sucked at selling and had to be politely asked not to come in on Monday. It wasn't glamorous, but being rejected ninety-nine times out of a hundred paid well, and the sales skills I picked up have continuously helped throughout my career.

—

I'm a sucker for the skills that working in sales can give you (especially if you are paid based on performance).

There is a salesperson inside all of us: the task is finding a product you love or believe in and selling it to the right people. I understand it is not for everyone, but you might find you have a knack for it. I didn't know I would be good at sales until I tried it.

These are some other skills that sales teach you:
- **Objection handling** – addressing concerns and questions that someone might have.
- **Rejection handling** – becoming comfortable with someone saying no to you.

The sales skills you pick up can also be applied during later job applications, interviews, negotiations and promotion opportunities. I don't want to cheapen it, but you must be able to convincingly sell yourself to a potential employer to score any job.

One small note about job applications: the resume

If you need a resume to apply for a job you want, I have only one tip for you: hire a professional resume writer to do it for you. Yes, it will cost money, but the investment will be worth it if you proceed to the interview stage and ultimately into the role. Many companies now use special technology to scan resumes and search for keywords. A human might only lay eyes on your application if it makes it through this filter. You might be competing against hundreds of other candidates. Every little advantage counts, and you don't want to miss out because of something you can fix.

If you cannot afford a professional resume writer, please use the available online resources. Also, always customise your resume for the specific role you're applying for.

Even if you never hear anything back after submitting your stellar resume—don't take it too personally. Ghosting is common, even if it is frustrating.

Another note about job applications: the interview

I'm not an expert at interviews, but I've done enough to uncover some strategies that help me perform to my best. I'll share three of my most reliable. The rejection may sting if you don't land the role, but you will still benefit from the practice. If you land the role, yay, but remember that you can decline it if it's not the right fit.

> *Prepare as much as possible before the day.*
> I go full-stalker mode on the company, discovering everything I can about them and the role. I check online for information from previous applicants on typical interview questions or tasks so I can practice them. If the interview is in person, I scope out the location and

plan how to get there. If it's online, I run through my tech and lighting.

Shake out the nerves in the hours leading up to it.
Going for a walk, jumping on the spot or listening to music calms and distracts me. I get hangry, so being fed and hydrated is a must. I remind myself my life isn't over if I don't get the job and that I'm not in a rush (so I don't need to vomit my words out).

Settle in first and then feel the room.
My only goal in the first ten minutes is to find my groove and warm up the crowd. For the rest of the interview, I'm dialled into what my ears and eyes tell me. If the interviewers are bubbly, I'll crank up my enthusiasm. If they are straight to the point, I'll put my game face on.

Me: *We have to break up.*

Boss: *You only started working here three weeks ago.*

Me: *When you know, you know.*

Boss: *But I thought you were the one.*

Me: *Don't say things like that.*

Boss: *I can change. Tell me what I need to do.*

Me: *Don't make promises you can't keep.*

Boss: *Is there someone else? Are you cheating on me?*

Me: *I knew I should have ghosted you.*

CHAPTER 7
THE CAREER SUPPORT TEAM

Ben grew up on a farm and has always been passionate about sustainability. Studying environmental science at university was, therefore, a natural progression. At the time he graduated, it was a notoriously difficult field to secure a job in. He didn't have the highest marks, but he did have an A+ personality. If he could just land in front of the right person, he knew he would be able to impress them. In the meantime, he continued working as a furniture removalist.

One day, as he loaded a couch into the truck, he started chatting with the owner. The topic came up about his struggle to find anything in the environmental science field. The owner happened to know someone who might be able to help him out. He connected the two, and within a month, Ben started his new job as an environmental consultant.

An epic career can't be built alone

We all need guidance and the occasional favour. We all need people to have our backs. We all need our own *Career Support Team*.

A Career Support Team is a group of people you surround yourself with to help you thrive in your career. A 'member' of your team could be a friend, partner or someone in your family. They could be a more professional acquaintance like a colleague, boss or mentor (I'll discuss mentors in more detail later). Regardless of who they are, what matters is that they're fully invested in your success. Not everyone in your life will make the cut. Some people give awful career advice, can't understand what you're going through or might not have your best interests at heart. You want to assemble an all-star squad, not a Tuesday-night social league team.

Don't worry; an induction ceremony for members is not required (though that sounds awesome). Nor do you have to create an official group and hold monthly team meetings. Someone might not even know they're a member. As long as you can count on their support, that's enough. By identifying who these people are (or the ones you need to find), you can have the support in place ahead of when you need it. If your house is already on fire, it's too late to purchase an extinguisher. Rather than spiralling into a panic when things don't go as planned in your career, you already have people you can trust to help put out any fires.

How a Career Support Team can help

Attempting to do a backflip for the first time on concrete is asking for trouble. Trying it on a trampoline, though? At least it will provide something to soften the landing if you mess up the flip. Members of your Career Support Team act like a trampoline. You're out in the world trying to perform career backflips, and they are right there beneath you, ready to catch you.

Tough times and whoopsies are going to happen. These members will have likely been through situations and struggles similar to the ones you're experiencing. They'll have felt frustration from being unable to find the right job or dealing with a demanding boss. Having people within reach as a safety net when venturing into the unknown can be reassuring.

There are two other vital functions your Career Support Team performs, which I'll discuss separately below.

1. Connect you with key people and 'secret' opportunities
There is a phrase that I recommend drilling into your brain:

Meeting one person can change everything.

Until the day I die, I will stand by the belief that the entire trajectory of your life can shift through one conversation with the right person. I've experienced it multiple times and heard countless stories backing it up from people like Ben.

Relationships (aka the people you know) are almost like their own form of qualification, another pathway to get you from A to B in your career. You can fill your resume with work experience and formal qualifications but still be unable to land an interview for the job you really want. Yet you could have one conversation with your mentor, and boom, they're introducing you to their cousin, who is hiring for that exact position.

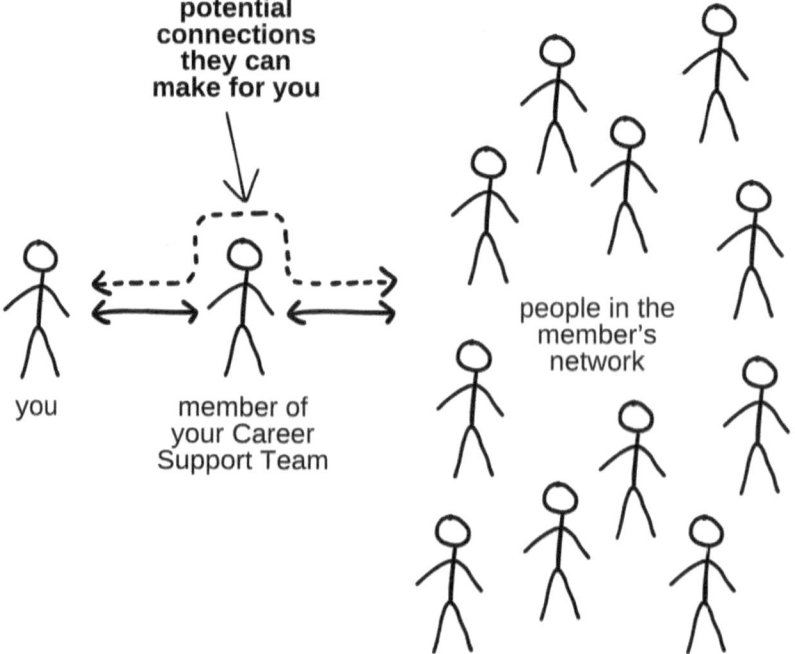

Not all job vacancies are listed online. Companies don't always seek applicants externally. There are loads of 'secret'

opportunities you will never see advertised publicly. If so, how do you even find out about or be considered for these opportunities? The answer is simple—you become the awesome person someone knows. It's generally easier, faster and cheaper for a business to hire someone who has been recommended rather than interviewing strangers. By building great relationships, you open yourself up to being the person someone thinks of when asked, 'Do you know anyone who would be good for this role?'

2. Encourage and inspire you to take risks

Have you ever had a great idea, one that gets you so amped in the moment that you can't wait to take action on it? Then your annoying brain finds all the reasons why it won't work. Or you run the idea by someone else, and they basically crap all over it. And before you know it, you've chucked the idea in the too-risky basket.

A great idea is most vulnerable during the brief period between its conception and deciding to take the first step. If you turn to the wrong person during this vulnerable phase, they may squash your idea, express unnecessary concern, or even make fun of you. If you keep the idea to yourself, you might never find enough courage to act upon it. But if you go to the right person, they will nurture the idea. They'll recognise that their opinion matters to you, and as such, they'll put themselves in your shoes. They'll be the hype person to get you over the line if that's what it takes.

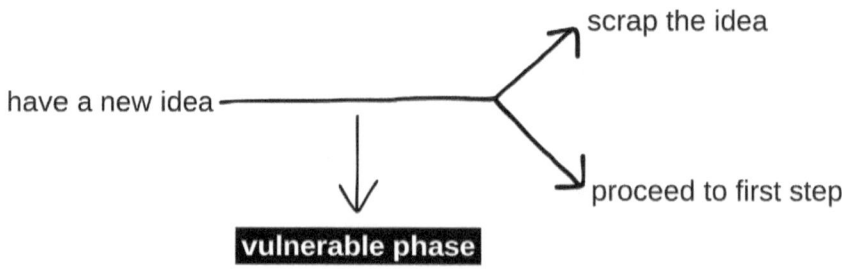

—

My boyfriend came home from his first day at a new job, labouring at a scaffolding company. I asked him how it went. 'I hated it.' he said. After three months of still hating scaffolding, he found a different job in an industry that excited him. He asked me what I thought. Knowing the new job would involve a significant pay cut, I was nervous. All he wanted at this moment was to hear that I had his back and we'd figure out the money together. Instead, I more or less said he should suck it up, that scaffolding would get better.

Thankfully, though, he didn't listen to me. He took the new job, loved every day and stayed for almost five years. After realising how much my reaction had crushed him, I swore to never let him down like that again. He was counting on me as a member of his Career Support Team.

The types of members you're looking for

There's no perfect number of members required for a Career Support Team. A nice balance of ages, experience levels, and industries is super beneficial. Initially, it's fine to have only one or two people you can openly talk to about your career and life aspirations. Building relationships with new members during this time will expose you to a wider variety of networks and experiences.

Below are four specific 'roles' I aim to have covered in my team. One member could cover multiple roles, and various members could fill the same role. The roles you want or need might differ.

Collaborator
- The kind of person who will workshop ways to improve your resume, rehearse interview questions with you or help design a website for the side hustle you've started.
- *'I will stay up all night with you to get this done if that's what it takes.'*

Celebrator
- Someone who will drop everything to share your wins with you. They'll praise you and tell you how proud they are, even about small things.
- *'FUCK YEAH, I KNEW YOU COULD DO IT!'*

Comforter
- They're always reliable in your moments of crisis. They can be depended upon to make you feel better when things go horribly wrong. When you're fed up with work, you can vent to them.

- *'Do you know what will make you feel better? Pizza. I'll order us one.'*

Challenger
- They're brutally honest, clear-headed and happy to call you out on your bullshit. The kind of person who thoroughly analyses the pros and cons of switching university degrees/apprenticeships/training courses.
- *'Great idea. Have you thought about <insert problem> though?'*

When there is a situation you need help with, ask yourself: *Who in my team can help me with this, or what sort of help do I need to generate the best outcome?* That way, you can seek out the person most likely able to assist you. In some situations, a close friend will be the perfect sounding board, while in others, your boss might be the person to go to. Other times, you might go to a parent seeking a Comforter when it's tough love from a Challenger you need.

Tips on mentors

Typically, a mentor is a person who uses their expertise and professional experience to accelerate your career growth. It's not that you want to become them, but rather that you want to learn from what they've done (or didn't do) and, in some cases, leverage their connections.

Mentors can be some of the most valuable members of a Career Support Team to find in your Casual Jog Years. I'll be honest: I found the concept of mentors intimidating after I left school. But as it turns out, some generous humans genuinely want to give their time to younger people or those with less experience. Who was I to stop them from helping me? I also realised it's not like a marriage proposal: I don't have to get down on one knee and ask this person to take my hand in mentorship forever.

If you feel awkward about finding mentors, don't worry, that's normal. The longer you are in your career, the more people you will come into contact with and the easier it becomes to form these relationships organically. In the meantime, the rest of your Career Support Team members are there to fill the gap.

Mentors can come from anywhere. The workplace is a great place to start. Mentoring programs or networking events run by your company, university or training institute can be useful. Social media and platforms like LinkedIn can also help you connect with like-minded people or those you admire. Keep an open mind and be ready to start conversations, even with strangers.

While travelling in Guatemala, I met one of my favourite mentors in a hostel dorm. She owned a business in Melbourne and was the first entrepreneur I had ever met.

We hit it off, and when we caught up back in Australia, a mentoring relationship naturally formed.

Here are some additional tips to kickstart your mentoring journey:
- Take the lead on communication and find a catch-up frequency that works for both of you. It could be coffee once a fortnight or lunch every six months. It could be a monthly Zoom. Or you could keep it more casual and reach out only when there's something you specifically need to pick their brain about.
- Maintain appropriate boundaries. Calling a mentor at 2am may be received poorly. Likewise, bombarding them with questions every second day might push it (unless they have explicitly said this is fine).
- The satisfaction of helping you might be enough, but always see if there is something you can assist your mentor with using your skillset.
- If the relationship is no longer a good fit or you've outgrown each other, you can always politely end it.

CHAPTER 8
SOCIAL MEDIA

COMPARISON IS THE WORST

Towards the end of university, I started driving for a food delivery app. Honestly, it wasn't what I had imagined I would be doing by that point in my life. However, it fit well with my study commitments, and the hours were flexible.

After collecting an order during a lunch rush, I waited at a pedestrian crossing for the light to turn green. As I glanced across the street, my stomach dropped. Standing on the other side was a girl I had gone to school with, dressed in a more professional outfit than anything I owned. I'd gathered from social media that she was doing well in her marketing career.

I know there was no reason to be embarrassed, but at the time, all that ran through my head was, 'Don't let her see that you're delivering food.' I looked down at the food bag and cursed under my breath. The company's logo stood out like a spotlight. I panicked. When the light turned green, I tried to hide the bag behind my back and rushed across the street. I mumbled hello to her and prayed for a human-size pothole to open in the road and swallow me up to save me from the embarrassment.

—

Don't worry; this chapter isn't a lecture about all the dangers of social media and how you should delete all the apps. Mainly, I want to talk about comparison. Even though you and I were raised in different generations, the natural instinct to compare ourselves to others is the same. While social media is an amazing tool for connection, inspiration and ideas, it has become a nasty hotspot for comparison.

Who are you comparing yourself to?

The pressure is very real when you are online and can see what other people are doing. You can immediately see what you don't have. It can make you feel as if your life isn't cutting it. The impact on your mental health can be massive, and it can add another level of anxiety around your career choices.

The ridiculous part is you compare yourself to people doing things you don't even want to do. I didn't want that classmate's job, but there I was, pining after it. This adulting thing is complicated.

If you're wondering why you automatically measure yourself against others, it's because your entire life, until now, has been compared to everyone else your age. When you were born, your weight and height were compared to the 'average'. That large part of your life called school? That's one giant comparison. But now, rather than being compared only during school hours, you have 24/7 access to keep the comparison party pumping. Yay!

Let's divide the people you might be comparing yourself to online into two categories:
- **People you know personally** – friends, family, people from school and work, loose acquaintances.
- **People you don't know** – influencers, celebrities, random people you follow (even though they probably wouldn't know your name).

Comparing yourself when you see an update from people you know has an additional emotional layer because it feels closer to home. It's easier to picture yourself as having what they have because you might be from a similar background.

The problem with viewing posts from people you don't know is that by the time you become aware of them, they're often already well-known or have a high follower count. They're automatically in the 'mystical unicorns' category (e.g. Taylor Swift). If you were only following one or two unicorns, you could probably scroll on by unaffected. But chances are you're seeing updates from tens, if not hundreds, of these people. Over time, this shifts the bar for what you compare your life and career to. You might feel flat because you assume you could only be happy if you reached their 'status', and the chances of doing that are slim.

At this stage of your life, where you choose to jog casually and take in the sights, social media will make you doubt yourself and your path if you're not careful. It is a stage where being more conscious of the platforms you spend time on and the people you follow is beneficial. Maybe set a time limit so you don't endlessly scroll. Maybe give yourself a pep talk before opening the app. Something like, *Hey, I'm awesome. I'm living my life, and these people are living theirs.* Or maybe take a total break to reset, then log in again if and when you're ready.

Comparing timelines

School was one big competition, and you were forever ranked and analysed against how quickly everyone else was learning. Your career is different. Everyone is on their own timeline. How long it takes you to do something shouldn't be compared to how long it takes someone else. It's easy to look at someone, see what they've accomplished and wonder why you're twenty steps behind.

Social media and the internet move *fast*. Sometimes, your career won't. Sometimes, you need to take it slow. Sometimes, it will take time to build the relevant experience to take the next step. Career goals can require patience.

It's normal to want to feel 'on track' when you leave school. The trouble is that you often end up on a track you don't actually want to be on. If you are making progress down a track for the sake of making progress toward *something*, you might be disappointed when you arrive at the end. *Oh wow, it turns out working fifty hours a week to get that promotion just meant my boss now expects me to work sixty hours.*

Career fan vs career critic
While you might be critical of someone else's career choices, you may find that you are even more critical of your own. It means that seeing someone else achieve something career-wise fuels your insecurities. The thing is, their success (or failure) says nothing about you.

Try to be happy when someone else has a career win. You can cheer them on from a distance. You can learn from what they've done, maybe using it as inspiration, but don't treat them as having everything you don't. Likewise, when someone else is having a tough time, you don't have to resort to thoughts about how you're doing way better than them. It's not a competition. Be a career fan, not a critic.

Social media as a career tool

Despite constant invitations for comparison, social media can be a fantastic career tool. There is a wealth of information on there, which can expose you to options you might not have known were possible. Social media itself is an industry you could explore. In today's world, companies rely on the power of social media for advertising and brand awareness more than ever.

I'll make a couple of points about being careful when using social media as a source of career wisdom:

> *People tend to show the good and hide the bad.*
> A lot of what people post online isn't accurate. So, while that podcaster only appears to record one episode a week, they might be preparing for ten hours, recording for five, editing for five and then marketing the episode for another twenty.
>
> *Social media gives you more of what you've already been looking at.*
> You watch one YouTube video on how a videographer made $10,000 last week, and suddenly, every second video on your feed is from another videographer talking about how to make money. It might make you think, *How did I not know about this? Is everyone doing this?* The answer is no. The algorithms on these platforms are designed to give you more of what you've already

shown an interest in. Be mindful of the rabbit holes you might go down.

Careers on some platforms can lean heavily in certain directions or industries.

LinkedIn is a perfect example of this. It's a professional networking platform. While anyone can technically be a professional, many members have a university qualification. This platform is great for recruitment and finding out what jobs are available (and in demand); however, there will be underrepresented industries or pathways, such as trade-based jobs.

Success and failure

When I was eighteen, I would have defined success as:
- Earning a lot of money.
- Having a job title that people are impressed by.
- Driving a nice car.
- Living in a mansion with a pool.
- Having a banging body (don't judge me).

This definition has changed since then as I have experimented with my career and life. If I'm having fun, doing work I'm passionate about and can fund my current life (while saving for the future), things are going swimmingly. I still have goals I'm striving towards, but I'm not letting them determine how I feel about my life.

What does success mean to you at the moment? What does it look like or feel like? What does failure look like? I am asking you these questions to make you aware of what you judge yourself against. You can't fail in this next stage of your life, but you will sometimes encounter failure. You might even want to label yourself as a failure. These feelings will be legit. But please, don't go around thinking you are a failure as a human being. That's just not possible.

If you take the Unserious Careers approach in these early years, there will be others around you who don't. This means that your attitude might be different, and your actions might not be the same as theirs. There is nothing wrong with that. Others might see what you're doing and be jealous, but never say it out loud. You keep doing what you're doing and allow them to do the same. If you see what they are up to on social media, cheer them on. Use what you see online as information and inspiration, not as an invitation to compare and doubt yourself. Focus on what you're doing.

CHAPTER 9
LIVE SOMEWHERE ELSE FOR THREE MONTHS
(ACTION)

Georgia wasn't a fan of high school. She took a gap year to give herself the time and space to decide what to do next. Halfway through the year, she moved to a ski field for the winter. Working as a ski lift operator meant plenty of days outside in the freezing cold, watching everyone else mess around in the snow. But she loved it and was surrounded by a great crew. On her days off, the ski field was her playground. Working there gave her clarity about what she wanted to do next. After an uphill battle finding an apprenticeship (unfortunately, because she was female), she landed one as an electrician. She now installs and maintains wind turbines.

—

This action has three main purposes:
1. Challenge your current ideas.
2. Gain exposure to new ideas.
3. Teach yourself life skills.

Remember when we spoke about the influences on your career all the way back in Chapter 1? This action will help you easily separate your ideas from someone else's.

By 'live somewhere else', I mean living somewhere other than the home or homes you have lived in while at school. It's a bonus if this is in a different city or country, but it doesn't have to be, as long as it is anywhere but your physical home. You can choose where to live and what to do with your time. It could be anything from living at your aunt's house to moving for university to backpacking.

I recommend three months because it is long enough to receive the benefits of the above purposes without costing you a fortune. It is enough time to give you a proper appreciation for living away from home and needing to fend for yourself without permanently moving out.

The career ideas you don't know about

Have you ever had the chance to interact with a hyperbaric welder? No idea what that is? I didn't either until someone told me these absolute beasts work underwater with fire, repairing things like oil rigs in the ocean. They're pretty much Scuba Iron Man (or Iron Woman). Are the chances high of you meeting a hyperbaric welder if you live inland, far away from any oil rig? No. But if you moved to a coastal area with an offshore station, you might bump into one at the supermarket. After hearing what they do, you might be all, *Holy guacamole, where do I sign up?*

Simply put, sometimes you need to move your butt to a new location to pick up some A-grade ideas. You need to expose yourself to alternative jobs, industries and career vibes.

WHERE YOU CURRENTLY LIVE

SOMEWHERE ELSE

Finding somewhere else to live

Two key considerations for deciding where you could live are your current financial situation and what you want to experience.

Your current financial situation
Living somewhere else costs money. It is far cheaper to live at home, provided this is an option for you. But on the flip side, the experiences you stand to gain in a relatively short time are far too valuable to wait five years or more. If you don't have the money saved to go travelling for three months (or you don't want to), you can look for options that cost less or allow you to earn money.

There are ways to minimise the costs associated with living somewhere else. If you can find an option where your accommodation is covered, that's ideal. Examples of this could be:
- Staying with extended family who are happy to take you in for free.
- Work-for-rent arrangements. This is common in hostels or campgrounds where you work in return for free accommodation.
- House sitting, i.e. moving into someone's house and caring for their pets while they're away on holiday.
- Working for a tourism company. Some companies will offer staff accommodation to attract people in locations where accommodation is difficult to secure.

- Working for a cruise line or on a super yacht.

What you want to experience

Your chosen destination doesn't need to be backed by a thoughtfully constructed pros and cons list. I decided to study abroad in the United States because I had grown up watching movies and TV shows about American colleges. You bet I wanted to drink from those red plastic cups, cook a turkey for Thanksgiving and shamelessly fan-girl the quarterback.

Use these ideas to inspire you about the opportunities you'd like to be exposed to and the locations that might offer them:

Seasonal locations.
Towns or cities that are busier in particular seasons often hire casual workers to fill positions. It could be beach or lake towns in the summer or mountain areas in the winter (like Georgia from the start of the chapter).

The best friend adventure.
Commit with a close friend to moving somewhere together for three months. This will give you the support of someone you know. It could be travelling, working overseas or moving to a seasonal town.

Moving in with one or more friends.
This might be where you stay in the same town but live in a share house with your mates. It can give you

more freedom than living at home without being too far away. Make sure you set up some friendship-saving boundaries from day one.

Extended travel or working holiday visa.
At the end of this chapter, I will give some specific tips about travelling. A quick heads up though, working holiday visas are one of the most cost-effective ways to see the world. These special visa types allow you to live and work in a foreign country. Twelve months is a standard visa length. To be eligible, generally, you have to be under the age of thirty. Any country that offers this visa will have its own restrictions, even about the type of work you can and can't do. This is the visa I used while working in Italy as a nanny in my gap year. It allowed me to fund my travels as I went.

Minimum stability

I hate to break it to you, but uncertainty in these first five years is almost guaranteed. Come to think of it, the uncertainty never stops. To cope with this, assessing the minimum amount of stability needed to function can be helpful. For you, it could be something like:
- **Decent wifi** – bingeing a TV show whenever the mood hits.
- **Friends** – hanging out once a week for a laugh.
- **Daily routine** – being in bed by 10pm.

- **Savings** – having enough money to cover your bills for a few months.
- **Reliable job** – knowing that your part-time position is secure while you decide what's next.
- **Backup location** – confirming you can move back home if it all goes to crap.

The minimum amount of stability you need might change depending on what's happening in your life. Maintaining this minimum level feels like juggling one less ball in the air while settling into the circus that can be adulthood.

Lifestyle and your standard of living

During these three months, you could experiment with maximising your standard of living. This means being strategic about where you live based on:

1. **Affordability** – how much it costs to live somewhere.
2. **Accessibility** – how much of what you want to experience is in the location.

New Zealand was a prime example of this for me. While the wages were lower than in Australia and the general cost of living higher, I wanted cool activities on my doorstep. The *accessibility* by living in Queenstown was high because of the mountains and the tourism industry. In contrast, I had a tight budget when I went on a best friend adventure in my early twenties. We went to Southeast Asia, where I could pay $5 per night for a bed in a hostel. The *affordability* was out the gate in that location.

Try living where what you want or might enjoy is accessible or affordable. It could be finding somewhere to work thirty hours a week instead of forty and still come out on top. It might be exploring what it's like to be able to swim at the beach every day rather than only on holidays.

Extra tips on living somewhere else

When you arrive in your new environment, observe the people around you—how they live, the kind of work they're doing and if there are any tasty work opportunities.

Adapt your expectations and be willing to sacrifice some creature comforts. I lived in a share house in New Zealand with seventeen other people. My room was the size of a shoebox, and the kitchen sink was forever stacked with people's dirty dishes.

If you're renting, you'll likely be doing things you've never done before, such as connecting utilities (i.e. electricity, gas, water, internet). You'll be winging it the first time, but your confidence will skyrocket once you've gone through the process.

—

I lived in a share house with two of my friends from university. Winter arrived, and none of us could get the heater started. We tried everything, but it wouldn't turn on. We called the landlord and asked them to have a heating specialist check it out. Jim, our saviour, came to the apartment a few days later. Within three minutes, he had solved the issue—none of us had thought to plug the heater cord into the electrical outlet at the wall. Oops.

—

Travel: yes or no?

Benefits of travel

To me, travel is the university of life. It is one of the most efficient and practical ways to learn about yourself and the world. I have worked my butt off in jobs so that I could afford it, and it is where I have poured any extra dollars.

Here are some benefits of travel:
- It inspires you by exposing you to new environments, people, foods and ways of living.
- It teaches you time management and how to think on your feet. You are forced to survive with only the items in your suitcase.
- It builds your confidence because things inevitably go wrong.

It's not for everyone, but I want to clarify that you do not need to be mega-wealthy to travel. With a bit of creativity and planning, it is available to anyone who wants it. You might not be able to book a flight to Tokyo tomorrow, but with planning and saving, it could be something you do in twelve months. There may be a reason why destinations or travel styles aren't accessible for you. The neat part about travel, though, is you can enjoy yourself just as much regardless of where you go or what you do.

What you should know before your first trip

If you're nervous about travelling, make it less complicated.
It might be helpful to choose an English-speaking destination (or one that speaks your native language). You might prefer to travel within your home country. Joining an organised group tour can be awesome if you want to grasp the basics and avoid booking everything yourself. Chat with a travel agent about your options.

Consider travelling with a friend (or a group of friends). This is an excellent option if you don't want to travel alone or need someone to give you the confidence to book the plane ticket. Double-check before committing that you're on the same page regarding what you want from the trip and your respective budgets.

Travel like the individual you are.
Just because your mates are going on a week-long party trip doesn't mean you have to. Your travel preferences are as individual as your career choices. Don't be afraid to lower your standards and rough it in the name of adventure! Taking the twelve-hour overnight bus instead of the two-hour flight to save money can be character-building.

Use your currency to your advantage.
If money is tight, travel somewhere cheaper, where your money goes further. In Paris, a hostel could be $75 a night. In Mexico, a hostel could be $10 a night. This might be a steal for you, but it can still make a big difference to the locals you support.

Don't go broke on your first trip trying to see and do everything.
Dip your toe with travel. A quick search online lets you know roughly how much accommodation, transport and food will cost you for almost any destination. It will allow you to budget accordingly and leave room for fun.

Please, please, please purchase comprehensive travel insurance.
This is a travel necessity, regardless of destination. If you don't have money for travel insurance, you need to keep saving because you don't have enough money to travel.

Friend: *We should totally start a business together.*

Me: *That might be the greatest idea you've ever had.*

Friend: *Right?! I can't believe we didn't think of it earlier.*

Me: *Imagine how fun it would be.*

Friend: *It'd be the best. What kind of business should we start?*

Me: *No idea. You?*

Friend: *No idea.*

Me: *Starting a business is hard.*

CHAPTER 10
THE FOUR—STEP DECISION LOOP

The tricky part about life beyond school is that there is so much you haven't even begun to think about. This is why we focus on the next five years in this book, not fifty. It's one thing to know the decisions you might need to make; it's another to know *how* to make them. The four-step decision loop is a process you can follow to help fine-tune your decision-making skills.

Step 1: Information – you learn something new or inspiration strikes.
Step 2: Individualise – you determine how this information relates to you.
Step 3: Implement – you use this individualised information to make a decision and take action.
Step 4: Interpret – you reflect and assess how this decision unfolded and use this to make adjustments or aid future decisions.

Here is an example of how this loop might look:

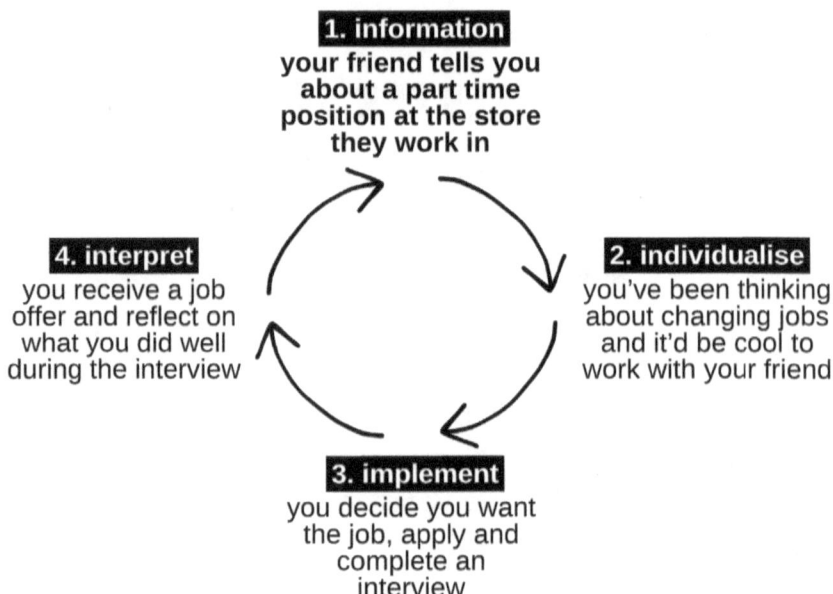

This four-step loop is a process that you repeat over and over again. With each repetition, you'll collect data and become more knowledgeable about yourself. It is a roadmap for learning better decision-making skills and bringing together all your weird and wonderful experiences.

Continuing with the example in the previous diagram, the loop can begin again:

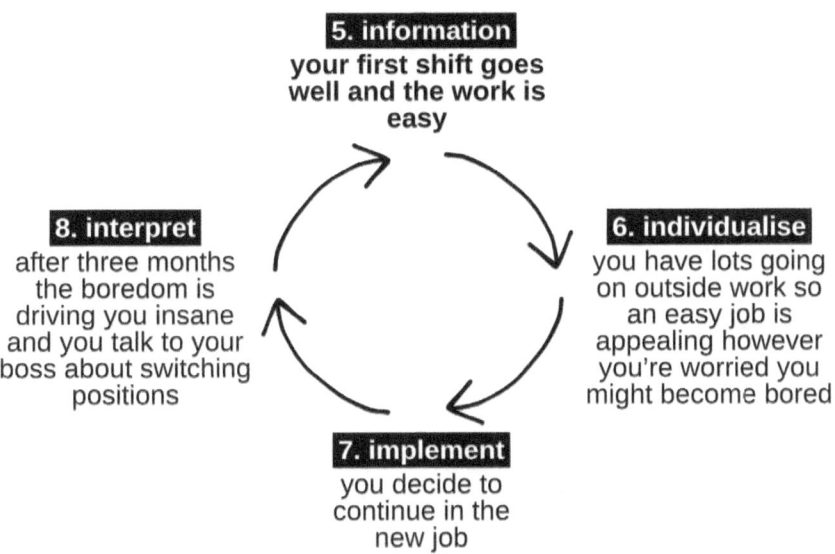

Let's dive into the steps a little deeper.

1. Information

Information can come in any form. You might be listening to a podcast and hear something fascinating. You might be chatting with a friend, and they mention a course they're taking. You might be in a relationship, and your partner is offered a job interstate. This whole book is information. Essentially, decisions are about choosing how to respond to new career-related information.

2. Individualise

This is arguably the most crucial step in the loop but is often overlooked, especially at school. It is easy to take a piece of information at face value and apply it straight to a career decision. However, this individualisation step is really about asking yourself: *How does this information apply to me? Does it even apply to me?* The more you know about yourself, the easier this step becomes.

You might want to become a computer scientist but then hear about how the tech industry is going through massive job cuts. It's enough to make you panic and look into alternative paths. Instead, you could ask yourself: *Does this information apply to me? How accurate is it? Is switching fields necessary, or could I continue down this path and ensure I specialise appropriately?*

The tools and actions in this book are designed to help you improve at individualising career information. That way, you're not relying on someone else (or the media) to tell you what to do. You'll be able to separate what information is worth paying attention to and what is background noise.

3. Implement

This step is simple—make a decision, then take the required action. You can spend these five years going around in circles, trying to make a perfect decision. But as I hope you have already picked up, sometimes you just need to make *a decision*. Get stuck in and see what happens. That brain of yours is wonderful, but sometimes it tends to overthink.

Saying no to an opportunity is still a decision even if you're not making any career changes. Don't forget to interpret these decisions as if you had made a change.

4. Interpret

You can't complete the loop if you don't analyse your career decisions to see how they've turned out. Is the outcome what you expected? What have been the upsides and downsides?

This reflection should be ongoing. Initially, it might be helpful to decide a time interval for when you first assess the outcome of your decision. It could be checking in with yourself after your first week at a new job or scheduling a discussion with your boss at the end of your trial period.

—

Once you have interpreted the results, you have valuable insight to help make future decisions or adjustments. Keeping a career journal of all your decision loops can be a fantastic way to keep track. Eventually, you can use what you uncover from your implementation and interpretation to 'mix and match' job ingredients. This could sound like:

I want to make a difference, but the emotional strain of working with disadvantaged kids is impacting my mental health.
Is there a job in the same industry but with less direct exposure to the heavy sides of it?

I like having an impact at a start-up, but having more certainty about my tasks would be nice.
Could you find a more established start-up where you will have a clearly defined role?

I love that I don't sit in front of a screen for hours as a plumber, but I don't like being outdoors during winter.
Could you find something that is based indoors but still active and hands-on?

Tools to help with individualisation and decision-making

Tool 1: Priorities

Personal values like family, community, respect and honesty went a little over my head at school. I got the gist but had zero idea how to apply the knowledge to my career decisions. So, let's talk about a more tangible tool for decision-making—your *priorities*.

Priorities are the activities, goals or projects most important to you at any given time. You're declaring to yourself: *These matter to me, and I want to commit time and energy to them.* For example, if you're still in school, one of your priorities might be to study and do well on your exams. Or it might be making the most of time with your friends before everyone goes their separate ways. After leaving school, your priorities might shift to finding a job you love, saving money, turning your band into a global phenomenon, etc.

If you're unsure what your priorities are, try this:
1. Flick back to Chapter 1 and find the diagram with a circle containing the different parts of your life (relationships, life admin, career, health, activities, community).
2. Choose one or two parts that feel essential (or exciting) for your Casual Jog Years. Even if you are set on becoming *<insert job title>*, you're allowed to have other priorities, too—don't be afraid to pick something unrelated to your career.
3. Break these parts down into specific projects or goals you can focus on initially. These become your priorities. *Using 'health' as an example, this might sound like, 'In the next three months, my priority is to sleep eight hours every night.'*
4. Whenever new information comes along, you can individualise it by referencing it against these priorities. How will it impact them? Does it align with them? Is it time to reassess your priorities?

After school, a priority of mine was seeing as many

countries as possible. However, doing well at university was a priority, too. Whenever the option to complete additional hours at my part-time job came up, I had to look at how this affected these priorities. Working more would give me extra money for travel, but it would also mean less time to study. The answer was rarely black and white, but knowing these priorities allowed me to weigh the options and decide more carefully.

The final crucial point is remembering to prioritise what matters to you, not someone else. Your sibling might track their daily steps like a psychopath because it matters to them, but it doesn't mean you have to.

Tool 2: Flip a coin

Have you heard of the coin flip test? It is where you use a basic coin toss to help you finalise a decision.

Say you can't decide between pizza or tacos for dinner. Here is how you would use the coin flip:
1. Assign pizza as heads and tacos as tails (or vice versa).
2. Flip the coin.
3. When you see which side the coin landed on, pay attention to your gut reaction.

If it landed on heads (pizza): are you happy and relieved? Or are you disappointed because you actually wish it were tails (tacos)? The coin flip is not locking in your decision; it is a test to show you which one you truly want.

THE FOUR-STEP DECISION LOOP

You can apply the same test to any decision in your career or life. Do you want to enrol at this university or that one? Do you want to study on campus or online? Do you want to study engineering or graphic design? Flip a coin and see what your gut reaction is.

If you feel meh about both decisions, this is an answer in itself and suggests you need to find other options. Or it could mean that you find a way to do both. How can you study engineering AND graphic design?

Let me repeat—the coin flip is not making the decisions for you; it helps reveal your feelings toward the options. You can use this to make decisions that you feel good about. Decision-making is a skill that you refine over time. The perfect decision rarely exists; sometimes, you only need to make a choice for *now*.

—

Making great career decisions is a skill that you can keep improving. Rather than going round and round about which decision is best, accept that you will probably make some terrible ones. But if you take the time to reflect (i.e. interpret) them, you will gather valuable lessons for next time.

CHAPTER 11
WORKPLACES

CHOOSE WISELY—THEY'RE A BIG DEAL

I arrived at the job interview expecting a professional environment. The first thing I noticed was that the office lady who greeted me didn't have shoes on—a huge red flag, given this wasn't a swimming pool. I ignored it and took the job anyway because I didn't know better. As it turns out, absent shoes were only the beginning.

—

I believe the quality of a workplace is the most crucial ingredient when determining how much you enjoy a job. You can enjoy the type of work you do, but if you do it in a terrible workplace, it will soon eat away at that enjoyment. Say you become a meteorologist (i.e. you forecast the weather) because you've always been fascinated by extreme weather events like cyclones and hurricanes. If your boss is hot-tempered, the office is always freezing, and a constant storm is brewing among your colleagues, it will impact your ability to enjoy the work.

Where you work will also dictate your exposure to opportunities. A larger company might mean you have more room for promotions. A smaller company might mean you can simultaneously work in multiple areas across the business. Make sure you give workplaces the credit they deserve in the coming years. You have the power to choose where you work as well as the power to influence workplaces positively.

Types of workplace cultures

In its simplest form, workplace culture is about the 'vibe' of working there. It is the atmosphere created by a bunch of people interacting in a shared space to achieve common goals.

Did you ever have that dream class at school, one that seemed to have all of your friends in it and a chill teacher? It may not have been your favourite subject, but the vibes were so good that you still gladly showed up. That's what it's like to be in a workplace with a great culture.

I want to give you some examples of the types of cultures you might encounter. I'll separate them into two groups:

toxic and healthy. You want to avoid entering workplaces with a toxic culture or speedily exit them and seek out the healthy ones. A workplace can be a blend of two or more. The culture naturally evolves, especially as staff change. One rotten apple can spoil the place, while one trustworthy leader can turn it around.

Toxic cultures
- **Blame culture** – people don't take responsibility when they mess up and look for someone else to point the finger at.
- **Gossip culture** – there is always drama and back-stabbing.
- **Customer-is-always-right culture** – a company that cares more about the customers than those who run the business (employees).
- **Sexist culture** – one sex is promoted or rewarded more often than the other.

Healthy cultures
- **Inviting or inclusive culture** – all staff members are treated respectfully.
- **Fun or vibrant culture** – you are encouraged to enjoy yourself and have a laugh.
- **Supportive culture** – everyone has each others' backs.
- **Growth-minded culture** – employees receive the tools to develop professionally.

Other cultures can be either toxic or healthy, depending

on your interpretation. A work hard, play hard culture is an example of this. It might be a workplace expecting you to grind, but you are rewarded with bonuses and staff parties when you hit targets. These can be fun to experience when you're young, but they might eventually become draining.

A quick note on colleagues
The funny thing about colleagues is that you're practically strangers thrown into a room together and told to be productive instantly. You'll often spend more time with these people than with your family, friends and partner. Colleagues can be a source of new friendships in these years. A mutual hatred for a customer is a pretty strong bond. Take your time to suss out the place before deciding who you might want to be friends with (if anyone).

Workplace red flags to watch out for

At that same workplace with the shoeless office lady, my much older male boss came to my desk on many occasions and massaged my shoulders. It was always done in a 'lighthearted' sense by him, but in hindsight, it was a form of sexual harassment. I know now I should have reported him and quit sooner, but I tried to dismiss his behaviour as harmless when it clearly wasn't.

—

Red flags are signs that could indicate more significant issues in a workplace, including a toxic culture. Here are some examples to keep an eye out for:
- Any form of discrimination, bullying or sexual harassment directed at anyone.
- High staff turnover (i.e. lots of people quitting).
- All of your coworkers are on edge when the boss is around.
- You are often not paid on time or are paid incorrectly.
- Unreasonable demands are made, such as doing overtime without appropriate pay.
- A boss puts you down or yells at you in front of other staff.
- Staff are paid minimum wage, but the boss flaunts expensive purchases.
- Boss complains to you about a coworker.
- Male-dominated workplaces where inappropriate and offensive jokes are the norm.

Not all red flags are conclusive evidence that it is a toxic workplace. Everyone can have an off day and make mistakes. Eventually, you'll become better at picking up on red flags that indicate this isn't a place you want to be for long. There might be obvious signs you can identify (like the shoeless receptionist), but the first signs are often based on a gut feeling. Trusting this feeling will save you stress.

A quick note on bosses
There is an expression that I have found to be accurate: 'People don't leave bad jobs; they leave bad bosses.' I have done it at least three times. People will quit jobs they love for no other reason than that they can't stand their boss. There is a power imbalance in the relationship, and shit bosses will exploit it. Some bosses are promoted without the talent to lead people effectively. While you can determine what not to do from a bad boss, I suggest seeking out good bosses in these early years of your career. They can take you under their wings and teach you what they know.

Working from home

Working remotely might be an option for you, depending on the avenues you're exploring. Or, working without physically travelling to an office or site might be impossible. Building someone else's home while sitting in your lounge room would be complicated.

I love staying in my pyjamas all day as much as the next person. But I must admit that I learned a ton in my Casual Jog Years by putting on actual pants and going to a physical workplace.

Organic learning happens in a physical work environment (with a healthy culture) that is tough to replicate online.

For example, bumping into your boss while making a coffee can be an invitation to ask them how they decided on their career path. Awkwardly washing hands in the bathroom at the same time as your coworker might be an opportunity to ask if they have five minutes to help you with a problem. If you work from home, your interactions with colleagues differ from those in a shared space. Making friends with your coworkers might be less common if they live in another city.

Regardless of your long-term goals, being involved in at least one physical workplace in these years is useful. You pick up additional skills that will complement working remotely if that is something you prefer to do long-term.

CHAPTER 12
WORK HARD AT ONE NON—CAREER ACTIVITY FOR SIX MONTHS
(ACTION)

Snowboarding seemed the polar opposite of something a nerd like me would do. I never thought I'd be coordinated enough to successfully (and safely) do it either. But it was one of the main reasons my boyfriend and I moved to the mountains in New Zealand.

Learning to snowboard was going to be hard work. It would be challenging because it was physically something I didn't know how to do. It would require consistent work over several weeks, months and years to advance above average. But I was willing to give it a shot. Naturally, I ended up in hospital with a broken wrist during my second lesson.

Seven weeks later, fully healed, I strapped back into the snowboard and started again. I spent most of the first season on my bum rather than upright. However, I was motivated to keep pushing because even on the roughest days, I still finished with a smile on my face.

You might have heard of the expression 'Work smarter, not harder'. There is some truth in it, but in my experience, the people who say it are either:
1. Still working hard; they're just smart about what they work hard at, OR
2. Worked hard for some time and can now sit back and reap the rewards.

With this action, I want you to question how you think about hard work. Why? So you can decide what you want to work hard at in your career (if anything). Hard work doesn't have to feel like a chore—it can be deeply satisfying. By testing your hard work limits with something you enjoy now, you can prove that you are capable of more than you thought possible. If there is ever a career goal that needs your all, you have evidence you can not only find another gear but also enjoy the process.

WORK HARD AT ONE NON—CAREER ACTIVITY FOR SIX MONTHS

Picking something to work hard at

It could be a hobby, a sport, learning a language or uplevelling your fitness. Anything you enjoy (or suspect you might) that you could see a return on the time you invest. It does not have to be physical, nor does it have to be mental. You might take DJ lessons or start singing at open mic nights. You could knit beanies (don't laugh—I've done this). It could be anything, provided you enjoy it and it is not currently what you do to make money.

I have specified six months because I've found it is enough time to see an improvement in whatever you're doing. Feel free to work on it for longer (or shorter if it makes more sense).

Setting a goal for what you want to accomplish in this time will be beneficial. If the activity is learning Spanish, your goal might be to hold a ten-minute conversation with someone who also speaks it. If you focus on making homemade pastries, maybe you want to master a cafe-worthy croissant.

Keep in mind that hard work is individual. You might find going to the gym every day easy, while another person struggles to do yoga once a month. Choose something that's both challenging and rewarding for *you*.

Finding your hard work sweet spot

During these six months, you can test your boundaries and discover your ideal *effort/reward ratio*. This ratio highlights what level of hard work is worth doing to get a desired outcome, i.e. your reward. For me, the relationship looks like this:

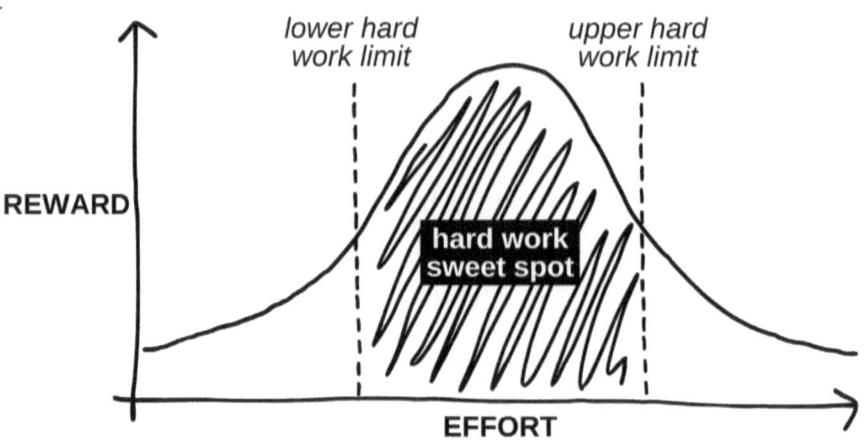

Lower hard work limit
The minimum amount of effort needed to push past your comfort zone. If you're only taking easy and comfortable steps, you're probably not working hard enough and won't receive much reward.

Upper hard work limit
The maximum effort you can put in before the reward is no longer worth it, or you push yourself too far. This is where you are at risk of burnout, injury or losing enjoyment of

the activity. Avoid working beyond this limit.

Hard work sweet spot
The hard work level between your lower and upper limits where you are healthily challenging yourself in a sustainable way. This is where you find your ideal effort/reward ratio. Spend your six months aiming to live in this hard work sweet spot.

On the first day of learning to snowboard, strapping my boots onto the board while sitting on the snow was easy, but I wasn't rewarded much for my efforts. Standing up without falling over was tricky but still not overly rewarding. However, once I started drifting slowly down the beginner's slope while holding my instructor's hand, I hit that *lower hard work limit*. I was concentrating and pushing myself, but I also felt like I was really doing it.

Over the following few hours, I played in the *hard work sweet spot*. Eventually, I could slide a short distance unassisted. Even though I was exhausted, I was enjoying myself while making progress.

I found my *upper hard work limit* at the start of the second day when I tried to impress my instructor by completing a left turn despite knowing none of the steps required to pull it off. Instantly, I fell, breaking my wrist and bruising my confidence. It turns out that if I wanted to be snowboarding for the long haul, I needed to stretch my limits safely.

Expanding your limits

The actions to stay within this hard work sweet spot will change as you continually improve and refine your skills. What was once complex becomes much easier (and potentially less rewarding).

Returning to the example of learning to speak Spanish, if you memorise ten new Spanish words every day for six months, you might be able to read restaurant menus. But you likely won't be able to hold a conversation unless you learn how to construct sentences and pronounce the words correctly. However, you'll probably feel overwhelmed if you jump right into watching a Spanish film without English subtitles on day one. You need to challenge yourself without overdoing it and giving up.

This is how your hard work limits might evolve in the first month:

	Lower hard work limit	Upper hard work limit
Day 1	Memorising ten new words.	Reading three sentences out loud from a Spanish book.
Day 30	Listening to a podcast in Spanish and picking up on words you recognise.	Ordering a meal in Spanish at a restaurant.

WORK HARD AT ONE NON-CAREER ACTIVITY FOR SIX MONTHS

By playing with these limits and gradually setting new ones, you build the belief that with the right motivation, you can put the effort into accomplishing your goals. You'll also trust yourself more and know when to slow down.

When you are testing your limits, you might feel uncomfortable and start thinking, *This is horseshit*. But once you accomplish the next milestone, it'll be more like *Crikey; what else can I do?*

—

Hard work is not compulsory, but you might need it to go places. If you don't want to work hard again, don't. Seriously. Nobody else can force you to work hard at anything. You might have to work a touch smarter or adjust your expectations, but you can still enjoy yourself. At least now, you will be in full control of that choice because you appreciate that hard work doesn't have to be a chore.

Me: *I reckon I'm a guarantee for that promotion.*

Colleague: *What makes you think that?*

Me: *The boss keeps giving me I'm-about-to-promote-you-vibes.*

Colleague: *But you weren't even selected for an interview?*

Me: *Yeah, but that's because they're playing hard to get.*

Colleague: *I think you might have the wrong idea.*

Me: *What would you know?*

Colleague: *Well, to start with, I am the boss. And secondly, your break was over ten minutes ago. Stop procrastinating and get back to work.*

CHAPTER 13
THE CAREER SUPERPOWERS

There's a sneaky word often thrown around when discussing careers that I want to call out—*potential*. Maybe you've been told before that you 'have so much potential' or you're 'wasting your potential'. It could be something like the academic potential to go to university, the creative potential to become an artist or the potential to become a professional athlete.

Potential is a dangerous word to place on a young person because it can often leave you feeling a responsibility not to waste it. What we should be focussing on instead are *career superpowers*.

Career superpowers are qualities or assets that you can deploy in your career to accomplish extraordinary outcomes. It could mean doing something ordinary but accomplishing it in record time. Extraordinary is defined by you.

Four career superpowers go swimmingly with the Unserious Careers approach. They are ambition, passion, attitude and purpose. While you may be unable to list these superpowers on a resume, they naturally make you stand out. They attract people to you, enabling you to build influential relationships over time.

This is what I love about these superpowers:
- They don't cost money.
- They don't require work experience.
- You don't need a qualification to access them.

Ambition

All Beth wants to do is create music and perform in front of an audience. Unfortunately, her rent and bills have other ideas. Music is a cutthroat industry, but she is determined to keep building connections, recording her tracks and releasing them into the world. She works full-time as a teacher during the week and plays gigs on the weekends. Being a teacher was never her dream, but it's a way to fuel her musical ambitions.

—

If you have *general career ambition,* you might be someone who simply wants to go places in their career. Perhaps it's making lots of money, climbing to the top of a company, starting your own business or being the best. You don't necessarily mind which industry or field this is in; as long as you have an outlet for your ambitious energy.

If you have *specific career ambition*, you might be similar to Beth. You're focussed on a particular *thing* you want to be successful at, and you're willing to go to great lengths to do it.

If you have *life ambition,* there might be hobbies and interests outside work that take priority over career goals. I've met many people with loads of ambition in the fitness space—people who run a marathon yearly or want to cycle across a continent.

Ambition is a career superpower because you naturally want to set goals, smash them, and then set higher ones. It will drive you forward and motivate you. It can also make you highly competitive. This isn't a bad quality, as long as you don't turn into that annoying person who always has to one-up everyone.

If you're ambitious, own it and follow it. If people have a problem with it, find people who don't. If you have places you want to go, be ready to pack your bags when any new opportunity comes your way. Don't hide your ambition because it will only lead to frustration. Find environments where your ambition is celebrated and rewarded, not asked to be toned down. Ambition is like fuel—it is meant to be burned.

Passion

During my fourth year at university, I found an opening for a twelve-month internship at a pharmaceutical company. The role was in procurement. I had no idea what procurement was; I still don't. Putting on my most charming smile, I blew them away in the interview with my 'passion' for the pharmaceutical industry and procurement.

A couple of weeks passed, and while knee-deep in exam preparation, I received a phone call from the recruitment department at the company. This was the happy news I had been waiting for. Screw you, study! The lady on the phone was delightful, and she said the interviewers were impressed with me; however—(nothing good ever comes up after that word). However, they could not offer me the internship because they doubted whether I even wanted to work in procurement. Busted.

—

For me, passion means you have real emotion behind something that interests you. I'm interested in carrots as a food, but I'm passionate about carrot cake. Passion can result from taking an interest and investing time into something to the point where you fall deeply in love with it. A passion can be broad (e.g. cars), specific (e.g. the fate of one fighter plane flown over France in 1942 during World War II) or anywhere in between.

It becomes a superpower for your career because you are infusing something you deeply care about into the activity you spend a sizable portion of your week doing. The thing about passion is you can't help but share it with others. When someone hears you talk about something you're passionate about, it oozes from every pore. Your passion is infectious even if the other person has no interest in the subject you're sharing.

From an employer's perspective, they can teach you skills to do a job, but they cannot teach you passion. It cannot be faked (as I tried to do in that procurement interview). When an employee is passionate about what they do, they go above and beyond to deliver for a customer.

You don't have to turn your passion into your career, but it can give you something to experiment with. While passion can keep you going through the tough times, it can also end up with you burning out and hating the very thing that once drove you. Deploy this asset carefully.

Attitude

After being in hospitality for a few years, Andrew decided to look for a carpentry apprenticeship. As he didn't know anyone needing an apprentice, he chose to get creative. His parents were signwriters, and he asked them to deck out the entire back window of his wagon with a sign. The sign read '21-year-old looking for a carpentry apprenticeship' and included his mobile number. It took less than two days for a phone call to come in with an apprenticeship offer from a carpenter impressed by his boldness.

—

I'll define the attitude I'm referring to: attitude is how you process and respond to problems, opportunities and changes in your career. Attitude is one of the career superpowers you can 100% develop or adjust at any time.

With the right attitude, you can do anything. A great attitude is usually positive, growth-minded and open to possibilities. You always try to find ways to make something happen.

A great attitude makes you more:
- **Resourceful** – using what is available to you, asking questions and seeking help when you don't know something.
- **Creative** – viewing situations in new ways to come up with unique solutions.
- **Bold** – willing to take a risk and understand that you'll still gain something even if it doesn't go exactly to plan.

Andrew is an example of someone with a great attitude. He was willing to think outside the box, use the resources available, and put himself out there to find what he was looking for.

With a terrible attitude, you will forever wonder why things aren't going how you want them to—and probably make excuses, too. You'll complain about problems rather than find solutions.

The people I have seen thrive are the ones who have accepted that they are responsible for their careers and that no school, employer, university, family, or friend is in charge of what they do. Taking ownership is an attitude.

Purpose

Laura is one of those people who lights up when you ask about what she does. She works in disability support and could not imagine doing anything else. If you have the time, she will gladly tell you about all the incredible activities that the people she supports have been up to that week. One week, they're sleeping overnight at the museum. The next, someone is preparing to be on a TV dating show for people with Down Syndrome. The path there took a few detours, but she always knew she would find her way to it.

—

The concept of purpose may sound way too deep, serious or confusing. That's normal. If someone had asked me when I was your age about my purpose, I would have asked if they were speaking German.

For me, there's a gateway question to talking about purpose which you may have already asked yourself: *What's the point?* Over the coming years, if you ever wonder what the point is, take it as a reminder to stop and reflect. *What IS the point? Is this what I want to be doing, or do I feel I have to?* When you do this enough times, you start to realise that you *want* there to be a point. This is when you contemplate purpose—a deeper meaning behind your life. Something you can fire up about that will drive you day in and day out. You might even discover that you have many purposes throughout your life.

Purpose is a potent superpower because it gives you energy and determination that any upcoming challenges cannot squash. You are focussed and sure of yourself. You aren't trying to be someone else. You are living life entirely on your terms.

Often, purpose can stem from personal experience or an event. Laura is an example of this. Her younger brother has autism. She has a strong sense of purpose and reason behind what she does in her career because of her experiences growing up with him.

My purpose is to have fun and inspire other people (like you) to do the same. It's not complex. It might even sound lame to you. But once I became aware of it through many years being way too serious, I couldn't ignore it. Without that purpose, this book wouldn't exist. I can't tell you your purpose. It happens, or it becomes clear.

If you already have a solid sense of purpose, an awareness of something you're here to do, explore it. But also know that even if you go off and do other things in your career, you can always return to it later.

It's ok to have no idea what I am talking about; this is only one of the superpowers. It's ok not to be driven by a purpose of wanting to help others. Suppose the point of working is to make money so that you can enjoy your life outside of work. Brilliant. Don't spend time chasing accolades that don't mean anything to you.

—

Career superpowers can be your most potent career assets. Everyone is rich in at least one of them. The trick is to experiment during your Casual Jog Years to discover which one (or ones) you possess. You might even find that yours change over time (for example, if you discover a new passion.) Use these superpowers to your advantage.

CHAPTER 14
MONEY

THE AWKWARD TOPIC WE CAN'T IGNORE

Wiremu is a proud Māori, and he became one of my closest friends at the travel company we both worked for. Like me, he was in his mid-twenties but by this age, he already had two children. His income was barely enough to support his family but you will never meet a guy more chuffed to hear how well you're doing than Wiremu. He wants you to win at life as much as he wants it for himself.

After being made redundant, Wiremu faced a harsh truth. Was he going to scrape by, or was he going to invest in himself and the long-term happiness of his family? He decided to use his passion and life experience by enrolling in a law degree. He is committed to providing a better life financially for his loved ones and better outcomes for other Māori families.

―

I have nightmares about receiving an email from someone who decided to blow all their money on a giant inflatable flamingo after reading these final two chapters. So, to be CRYSTAL CLEAR, this chapter and the next are not financial advice, nor am I a financial expert. Everything here is for information purposes only: please do your own research.

Money will absolutely have an impact on your career. While it might be an awkward topic, it's not something you need to fear. Financial stability is necessary, but it doesn't mean you must centre all your career decisions around it. You still need to prioritise your health and happiness. This chapter is me gently opening the money can of worms with you.

How accurate are your income expectations?

Growing up, I rarely had detailed discussions about money with my parents. I knew we had enough money to buy fish and chips on Friday nights but not to eat at a fancy restaurant. After moving out of home, I quickly discovered that *everything* costs money. It turns out the cheeky buggers hadn't been entirely honest about just how much it costs to breathe.

As you move through these years, it can be helpful to start questioning your ideas around money and where they might have come from. What were the conversations around money like in your family? Were there any? Were you shown how to save and invest? The way money is presented will influence your expectations around how much you earn and the lifestyle you want to have.

Based on your current loose career ideas, pick a number you could expect to earn per year at the end of your Casual Jog Years. You can do some research if you need to. If you are debating whether to become a stonemason, you could Google 'What is the average salary of a qualified stonemason?' You could also find job listings with an estimated salary or hourly wage.

Now that you have this number, what does it represent? What kind of life will you be able to afford? Maybe it allows you to save for a house, move out of home, buy a nicer car or help a family member out.

I don't want to ruin your money fantasy, but have you factored in tax yet? What about a student loan if you went to university? Using approximate Australian figures, if you earned $80,000, you might be left with $63,600 after tax. If you have a student loan, that number might come down to $60,400, give or take. Ouch.

The thing about income expectations when starting your career is you don't have any context for what that amount of money means or how far it will stretch. It's almost the same as Monopoly money. Suddenly, you're earning a full-time wage, and it's more money than you've ever made. And you think, *I'm rich, let's go!* Then the realisation sinks in that there are many living costs you haven't factored in.

Income trade-offs
Certain fields or jobs can come with a form of *income trade-off*. An income trade-off is when you compromise or sacrifice a higher wage for something else you value. Here are three examples:

> *Working in the public sector (i.e., for the government).*
> - This might involve compromising a higher wage for increased job security or more attractive benefits.
> - An accountant who works for the state treasury department may earn less than someone in the same role at a private accounting firm.
>
> *Working for charities or not-for-profits.*
> - This could mean sacrificing a higher wage for the satisfaction of helping a cause.
> - If you're drawn to this sector, often it's because you're passionate and want to make a difference.
> - Tighter budgets (especially if they rely on donations) might mean earning less money in return.
>
> *Working in the arts or creative fields.*
> - This might mean compromising a higher or more stable wage to work in a field you love or in the hope of making it big.

- Your income may not be consistent or predictable. You also may need to do unpaid work or volunteer to 'break in' to the industry.

If you work in these environments, you essentially agree to play the game by these unofficial rules. However, you still have a choice in what you do with your money. You can learn more about budgeting, saving and investing. You could supplement your earnings elsewhere, e.g., freelancing, building an online business, or investing. You could also stay in these environments for a certain length before transferring your skills to an industry where you can earn more.

Learn how to budget ASAP

One of the best investments you can make in yourself is learning how to manage your finances. Budgeting involves working out how to spend less money than you earn. When you do this, you are living within your means. If you spent $507 last week but only earned $426, you have a problem. If you spent $426 but earned $507, there is $81 that you could save or invest.

BUDGETING MADE SIMPLE

money coming in *is more than* **money going out**

- income from work
- government payments
- money from family
- scholarship payouts

spend now *plus*
- living costs
- food
- transport
- social activities

save for future
- invest
- emergencies
- bigger items
- adventures

These next five years aren't likely to be the highest earning years of your career, especially if you are studying full-time or earning an apprentice's wage. You might earn more than you did while you were at school, but generally speaking, you will likely be making more per year when you're forty than twenty. All this is to say that the better you become at budgeting, the less stressed you will be.

It sounds simple on paper, but budgeting can be complicated in real life, especially if you don't believe you're good with numbers. Financial companies will present products to you, which might seem a sweet deal but can be debt traps. The potential dangers of items like credit cards, car loans and buy-now-pay-later services are worth reading about before signing up for them.

When you have budgeting down pat, saving money becomes infinitely more achievable. You might not be a bad saver; rather you might have some sub-par spending habits. When you build up some savings, you will be far more prepared to deal with unexpected costs. You can also save for exciting items and experiences.

I wish I could tell you that you can have everything you want in these years, but chances are, you won't be able to afford it all. You might have to make sacrifices. Focus on building sustainable saving and spending habits while enjoying yourself.

Investing and the power of compounding

While this is not a book about how to become rich, I want to introduce the idea of investing. You can then sneak off and do your own research (which you could do while learning how to budget and save!) If you struggle with maths (or it bores you), that doesn't mean you can't invest. Try to stick with me during this section and re-read it if needed.

Here is one way to differentiate between saving and investing. Saving is setting aside money today so you can use it in the future. Investing is putting money somewhere today so it will grow and you can have *more* money to use in the future. Investing builds wealth and is like saving for the future on steroids.

Compound interest is one magical mechanism through

which investing can grow your money. Say you have a spare $1,000 and are happy not to see the money again for the next twenty years. You go to your bank, and they offer to put your money in an investment account with an annual interest rate of 10%. Every year, they will pay you $100 in interest (10% x $1,000). However, not only will they pay this $100, but they will also pay you 10% interest on the interest you earned in previous years. You earn interest on interest on interest on interest (and so on). The interest is *compounding*. The graph below demonstrates this impact over the long run:

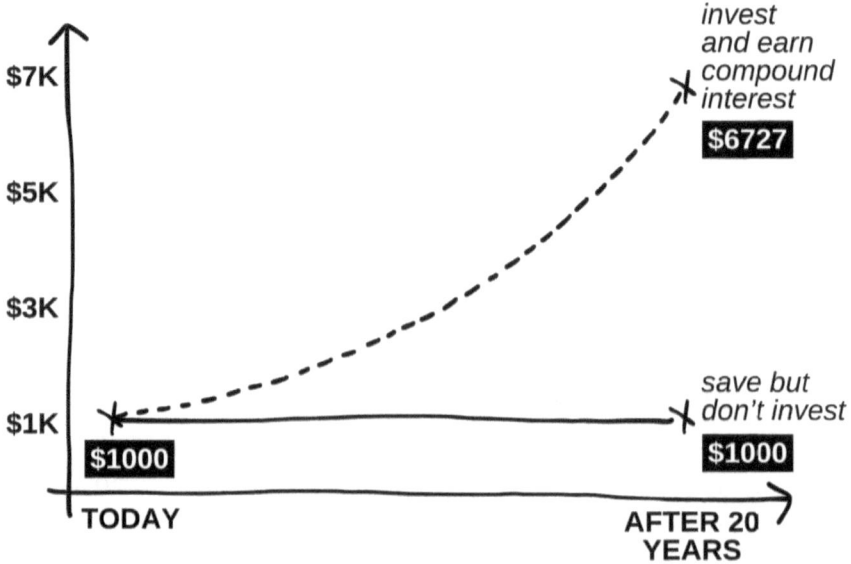

Through compound interest, that initial $1,000 grows to $6,727 over twenty years with no additional effort from you.

MONEY

Whereas, if you had only saved $1,000 without investing it, in twenty years, you would still have $1,000 (and because of inflation, you would have been able to purchase less with this money than you would today).

—

When it comes to money, you may feel like you aren't making much progress in your Casual Jog Years. But everything you invest your time and energy in is continually compounding—all of the actions and suggestions I've made in this book compound. The people you meet, skills you gather and experiences you have are all building on top of one another. You have to give yourself enough time to see the benefits of these investments. In the meantime, do yourself a favour and become a champion at budgeting.

CHAPTER 15
SAVE $500 FOR A SUNNY DAY— AND SPEND IT
(ACTION)

A group of four mates started a shared bank account after high school. They still have it to this day, over fourteen years later. Every week, each of them pays $10 into the account. The payments are automated, so they don't have to think about it.

    4 guys x $10 a week x 52 weeks = $2,080 saved per year

The idea is that these funds pay for a boys' weekend away every year. $2,080 can go a looooong way in one weekend.

—

As I said in the previous chapter, learning more about money is something everyone should do after they leave school. While saving and investing are important skills to build, there is something equally important to learn: how to enjoy your money. I'm talking about spending strategically on things that give you crazy levels of fun for your investment.

If you get too serious about your financial future too soon, you miss what's happening *now*. You also lose sight of the point of working and making money. Stressing about rising house prices as soon as you leave school is probably not the best use of your mental energy. You've barely had a chance to earn money consistently, let alone prepare yourself for the commitment of having a mortgage.

This action is about saving $500 for a Sunny Day and understanding how to spend when the sun shines. I appreciate that it might not sound super career-focussed, but hear me out. If the other actions still somehow felt a bit serious, this is one I insist you HAVE FUN with. I left this action until last to remind you about the value of being unserious and that work is one part of your life.

What is a Sunny Day?

Ever heard the expression 'Always save for a rainy day'? Basically, it means putting money aside for when shit hits the fan in your life. That might be your car breaking down, an unexpected medical bill or replacing your phone after it went for a ride in the washing machine. A Sunny Day is the opposite of a rainy day: you use the money you've saved to have a great time.

A Sunny Day can be an experience or an item that brings fun into your life. You're after something you don't have to invest a significant sum in but will receive a thrill from. I can't tell you exactly what a Sunny Day is for you. It will be something that you value, which might be different from me. For example, I love cooking, eating, and, I guess, food in general. Spending $500 on shoes doesn't tickle my fancy, but treating myself to a seven-course feast does.

Here are some Sunny Day examples:
- Going out for a decadent brunch.
- Spending two hours at a day spa.
- A weekend getaway with your partner.
- Catching a sporting event live with your friends.
- Hosting a birthday party with loads of snacks.
- Buying a new video game and giving yourself a whole weekend to play it.

Sunny Days are excellent at teaching you how to live. They ensure you keep in mind what matters to you. They make you happy. For me, they are what I am working for. They are the greater purpose of the money I make—the highlights of my life. You uncover what you want from your career by figuring out what you enjoy doing outside work hours.

A career is how you can make it all happen. Sunny Days should be the reason your career exists at all.

The coolest Sunny Day I've had was in New Zealand. I bought a fifty-year-old bright blue boat with three friends. We each put in $500 and spent the following three summers cruising and wakeboarding on the lake. Who said owning a boat was only for the rich?

Start your Sunny Day Fund

There are a few reasons why I suggest saving $500:
- You could save for it in a year by putting aside $10 every week (less than the cost of most fast food meals).
- It's enough to do something big with or many smaller things.
- If you're not confident with money now, it's a simple goal to focus on.

However, you can absolutely make your Sunny Day Fund smaller or larger, depending on your unique circumstances and financial situation. I repeat: this isn't financial advice. Please don't sue me.

Sunny Days aren't about throwing away money with an attitude of, *Fuck it, I'll never be able to afford a house anyway.* They are about intentionally saving and then spending money on something that lights you up. A Sunny

Day Fund is the bomb because you don't specifically have to know what you're saving for. All you need to do is trust that Sunny Days will inevitably come up in these five years. You will have less reason to say no when a tempting idea comes your way.

I purposely say 'save $500', not 'chuck $500 on your credit card' (if you have one) or 'ask for $500 from your family' (if this is an option). When you have saved the money, you can revel in the Sunny Day when it comes. You don't owe anyone else for it. It is yours to savour.

How do you save for a Sunny Day?

To save for a Sunny Day, you need to confirm that all your bills are covered and you have some savings for emergencies (i.e. rainy days). In my early twenties, I tried to have at least $1,000 readily available to pay for anything unexpected. A Sunny Day Fund is for a particular purpose; it differs from the savings you hopefully build for emergencies or more expensive purchases.

Sunny Days don't have to cost a lot of money. Let's pretend you put aside $10 weekly from your part-time job. Six months pass, and you hear your favourite band is playing a show in your closest city. Tickets are $100. You check your Sunny Day Fund—$260 ($10 x 26 weeks). You buy the ticket, convince some friends to go, and you all have a sensational time.

That's a Sunny Day. You don't have to wait until your fund has hit $500 to spend it if an incredible opportunity pops up.

You might spend all your Sunny Day Fund on one thing every three years or a smaller portion every three months. How and when you spend is up to you, as long as it is meaningful and intentional.

Here are some ideas on saving and making the most of Sunny Days:
- Start small and build the habit of saving for both rainy and Sunny Days. Keeping it sustainable is better than being too ambitious and quitting after a month.
- Consider what you are already spending small amounts of money on each week that you can cut back on and save instead. It could be something as simple as a can of Red Bull.
- Invest in experiences and yourself. It could be a $20 dance class that makes you sweat and smile for an hour.
- Keep your calendar open. Clear your schedule when necessary. Make room for fun and spontaneity.
- Be fine with periods of temporary broke-ness. You have your whole life ahead of you. It's ok if you aren't rich or purchasing your first property by age twenty-three.
- Mooch home-cooked meals off your parents as much as they'll allow you to (in your first five years, it's expected).

- Only let your holiday (annual) leave build up in your first five years if you have an outstanding plan for it. Use those days instead to recover from that concert, flesh out a sick business idea with your mate or find your next rad job.

Compound enjoyment

In the last chapter, the investing concept of *compound interest* came up. A similar concept can apply to experiences in your twenties. We can capitalise on *compound enjoyment*—the ability to reminisce about the sweet things you did over and over again. It's not living in the past; it's enjoying what you have done even after it ends. I still tell stories about adventures in my late teens and early twenties. They're a gift that keeps giving, and these experiences continue to influence my career decisions.

The cost of fun is often less in these first five years because your expectations are lower and your tastes are cheaper. Fun should not be sacrificed or saved only for the future. Making time for it now will mean you're more likely to keep having fun because you've built the habit.

I believe you have a greater chance of experiencing something legendary by saying yes than by saying no. 'Yes' should be your default in these first five years so there is less hesitation and more buzzing about what you could experience. Of course, saying yes should never put your personal safety or mental health at risk. It should always align with your beliefs and priorities.

When you invest in enjoyment now, these moments can build on one another in the long run. This can improve the overall fulfilment of your career and life. One of the fundamental flaws I see in retirement is the idea that we start working and don't stop for forty years or more. We then hope that when retirement day comes along, we actually like it. What a giant risk to take with our lives. I say screw that and enjoy ourselves along the way.

Me: *Listen, we need to talk about my raise.*

Parent: *What raise? I don't even pay you a wage.*

Me: *Precisely my point.*

Parent: *But I put a roof over your head, food on the table and clothes on your back.*

Me: *And I appreciate that, but as the most valuable asset to this organisation, we both know you can't afford to lose me.*

Parent: *Did you just call our family an organisation?*

Me: *Yes, and I would hate to see this organisation suffer because you didn't pay me enough. So, about that raise.*

CONCLUSION
BEFORE YOU START YOUR CASUAL JOG

There's a photo of me standing at the airport in front of the International Departures sign. I'm about to say goodbye to my family before I board a plane and start my gap year. You can tell I am shitting myself. I'm clutching my bag a little too tightly, my cheeks are flushed, and you just know there are sweat patches under my arms.

The look on my face suggests I am questioning every decision I made to get there. But if you look past the awkward smile, terrible haircut and dorky glasses, you can see a hint of something else—

Excitement.

As much as I am terrified about walking through the departure gate alone, I cannot wait to see what else is out there.

The final pep talk

I'm not great at goodbyes, so let's not make this weird.

This book is here to inspire you. Hopefully, it has given you more confidence to tackle your career in these next five years.

You do not need to do everything that I've suggested. Prioritise and apply the actions that feel right for you. Continue challenging your way of thinking.

Your career is an adventure. You choose where you go and what you do. You don't always know where that will take you, but that's the exciting part. It might be somewhere even better than you imagined.

You're not going to make perfect decisions all the time. You'll fall and discover how to pick yourself back up. When you have done this enough, you start to appreciate the environments and circumstances that you thrive in. You can recognise the actions that led to excellent outcomes and vice versa.

Ask for help from those around you. You're not expected to have all the answers.

You're on your own timeline. Take your career at your own pace. This is a time to casually jog and take in the sights rather than sprint to the end.

BEFORE YOU START YOUR CASUAL JOG

Experiment with work and explore what it means to you. Change your mind a thousand times. Accept that there are going to be good days and bad days.

Be kind to yourself over these five years. Celebrate the mini and major milestones along the way.

You don't have to love what you do for work, but please don't settle for something you hate. Your career is only one part of your life; don't forget about the others.

Whenever you find your career getting too serious, do something unserious. Something fun.

Don't underestimate the power your career has to create an epic life.

Take ownership.

Start with one action.

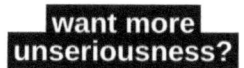

you know what to do

ABOUT THE AUTHOR

Alana Kilmartin is an Australian author and speaker who grew up on a farm outside a small town you've probably never heard of. She graduated from Monash University with a double degree in Commerce and Biomedical Science. Shortly after, Alana moved to New Zealand and became the number one travel agent in the country. The burnout and quarter-life crisis that followed inspired her to write Unserious Careers. Alana currently lives in Melbourne.

www.ingramcontent.com/pod-product-compliance
Lightning Source LLC
Chambersburg PA
CBHW032036290426
44110CB00012B/832